WHAT TO DO WHEN
'THERE'S NOTHING TO DO'

*

A book for every busy mother with children
under five. It is a collection of nearly 600 ideas
for parents, all of them involving little or no
cost, which provides nearly 600 answers to the
problem of what the children can do when
'There's nothing to do.'

Members of the Staff of
The Boston Children's Medical Centre
and Elizabeth M. Gregg

What to do when
'There's Nothing To Do'

Foreword by Dr. Philip Evans, M.D., F.R.C.P.
Senior Physician, The Hospital for Sick Children,
Great Ormond Street, and Director of the Department
of Paediatrics, Guy's Hospital

Illustrations by
MARC SIMONT

ARROW BOOKS

ARROW BOOKS LTD
178–202 Great Portland Street, London W1

AN IMPRINT OF THE  HUTCHINSON GROUP

London Melbourne Sydney
Auckland Johannesburg Cape Town
and agencies throughout the world

*

First published by
Hutchinson & Co (*Publishers*) Ltd 1969
Arrow edition 1971

*Made and printed in Great Britain
by The Anchor Press Ltd.,
Tiptree, Essex*

ISBN 0 09 004490 8

Contents

Foreword

Publications for parents

This book will be welcomed by every parent who hears the familiar plea: 'What can I do?' Many helpful answers are described here but the appearance of this volume has a greater significance. It is the result of collaboration between a large publishing house and a world famous medical institution—the Children's Hospital Medical Center of Boston, U.S.A.

Obviously there are many other subjects about which parents would like advice, and the project aims at producing a series of books and booklets on all phases of child growth and development. Doctors, social workers and nursery school teachers, or writers working closely with them, will write the books. A review board of doctors from the hospital's staff will consider each before it is published. The Hospital's Department of Health Education has established an editorial office for this work. When a volume is to be brought out in another country the text will be revised to meet local needs.

I wish the British version of this admirable project

the success it deserves. Mental and physical well-being depend on a good start in childhood and that is where Health Education begins.

PHILIP EVANS, M.D. F.R.C.P.

Senior Physician, The Hospital For Sick Children, Great Ormond St. and Director of the Department of Paediatrics, Guy's Hospital

Introduction

The home can be a battlefield or it can be a domestic factory where each inhabitant lives a happy productive and constructive life according to his or her stage of development. There's everything in the average home for the youngest member even if he or she doesn't at first use every article for the purpose for which it was intended. With guidance a child's play activities can be matched to the appropriate stage of development.

The staff at the Boston Children's Hospital Medical Center have skilfully applied their knowledge of child development to the universal problem of the busy mother who has to keep her offspring safely and busily occupied when there's housework to be done or bad weather keeps them cooped up under her feet indoors.

The nursery school teachers, in particular Elizabeth Gregg, doctors, nurses, librarians and other workers in the field of child care have pooled their play 'recipes' to produce an illuminating handbook for mothers, grandmothers and aunts. 'What to do when there's nothing to do' is far from being just a guide to a rainy day; it offers ideas for play from infancy to five years, using all the simple oddments which can be found in every home.

The book establishes a child's need to explore, his right to test his physical capacity and discover his body in relation to the space around him. Through the play programme which his mother can provide from the simple home environment his 'messing' has a purpose and can be a step towards other important learning— vocabulary building, self-confidence, the joy of knowing. Imaginative play with miniature objects, toys or puppets are the child's first venture into what will be his social world. As he grows older he learns to master materials and create reproductions of what he sees adults make and do.

The book is a text on child development as well as a manual of helpful suggestions to parents about how they can enrich their child's play and their own daily home life.

I

What to do when
'There's nothing to do'

What mother has never been confronted by that plaintive upturned face (or several of them), stating flatly, 'There's nothing to do, Mummy, there's nothing to *do*'?

More often than not, the demand reaches its highest pitch on just those days when everything else is awry. The rain is pouring down. A mother is behind in her work, the supper still to be planned and cooked. She's tired and pre-menstrual and, wherever she turns, a discontented child is underfoot.

This book was started with just those days in mind. Children, especially pre-school children, have an emotional radar for sensing a mother's flagging spirits and will go to all lengths to keep themselves at the centre of her attention—just at the moment when she is short of energy and ideas.

Sometimes, however, the complaint of nothing to do comes when a mother is feeling energetic and imaginative and inspired to create. So, as this book grew, we added play ideas for brighter days when mothers have a little extra time to do something with their children.

For the benefit of mothers, we chose ideas that would be practical, simple to set up, and usually would not require undivided attention or help. Mothers are not nursery school teachers and should not expect themselves to be; they have other things to do besides playing with their children. Most of the 'toys' described in this book can be made from everyday materials which usually are on hand in any household and cost little or nothing. For what good would play ideas be to a busy mother if she has to drop everything to shop for special materials?

With the child's development foremost in mind, we have selected ideas to match as nearly as possible what is known about the particular needs and interests at different ages. Child specialists now seem to be concentrating their research on the very early years, particularly the first year of life, and before very long we will know much more than we do now about how children learn, how they develop mentally and what interests them most. Then we'll be able to add more play ideas to this book. In the meantime, our present knowledge of child development, while far from complete, is sufficient to let us be quite specific about certain matters.

In this book we have tried to give concrete answers to various important questions: What rests a baby? What interests him? When does he learn to grasp something and let it go? When do children stop throwing blocks and begin building with them? At what age is 'messing around' with clay and mud especially valuable and why? When has a child enough co-ord-ination to use blunt scissors?

Until very recently, babies were overlooked as 'players'. What kept a baby happiest, it was thought, was food, cuddling and quiet. But now studies of early infants show that they are eager to play, and learn very quickly by touching, looking, listening. These activities are their 'play'. Their 'toys' are simple but none the less important for being so. Research seems to be confirming the old idea that earliest childhood is the period of greatest learning.

Recognition that learning begins in the cradle does not require us, however, to bombard two-year-olds with school primers or see how much of our adult knowledge we can thrust on a child as early as possible. The child's way of learning, about which we still have a great deal to discover, is different. His logic is not an adult's logic, his order not an adult's order, and he should have the freedom to learn in his own way. To some grown-ups, certain play ideas in this book may seem downright silly—tearing up newspapers, splashing water, or dumping tins on the floor. 'Doing' is a child's way of experimenting with his world. It is not important to him to produce a 'thing' in the adult sense. He needs the opportunity to use his own unique drive to master and to create.

A young child probably prefers 'home' toys, such as pots and pans, tins and cartons, to shop toys. These things are part of his daily life and he longs to reach out and experiment with them. Moreover, he sees his mother using them, so he wants to use them, too. 'In the everyday experiences of the child', said Jean Piaget, the Swiss psychologist, 'lie the origins of curiosity.'

A baby's random movements and a child's seemingly aimless activities are his earliest methods of learning. A baby watching a mobile is exploring with his eyes. A two-year-old tearing papers, besides developing his hand co-ordination, is testing his mastery of his environment and satisying his curiosity about materials. What do we mean when we say that an adult is creative? Only that his work exhibits the application of an unusual inventiveness to an unusual curiosity. There is a sense of play involved. The spirit of the backyard, mudpies, and lopsided structures of junk isn't very different from the spirit of a physics laboratory, an artist's studio, or an architect's drawing board.

Anyone who has closely watched a child at play quickly recognises he is in the presence of hard work. Play is a child's work, and he approaches it earnestly. The toddler sits digging in the hard earth with a metal spoon, scraping and scooping until the spoon strikes a large stone. He may spend an hour digging all around the stone with his spoon or he may get the garden trowel and solve his problem in five minutes. Basically, his task is the same as the problem-solving that confronts adults. They have to solve their problems in a more complex world, but the foundation of approaching and mastering problems often is laid on the problems of their childhood.

In play a child learns bit by bit what the world is —what is wet, what is dry, what hurts, what he can lift and push aside, what make things stop and go,

hold together, fall apart, and what jobs require outside help. He experiments by feeling, smelling, tasting, dropping, kicking, messing, and watching. Play is also a good outlet for troubled feelings and overflowing energy. In games with other children, a child meets

rage and attack, but also laughter and a sense of be-
longing. In play a child faces many of the crucial tasks
of living. Just as his earliest relationships with his
family colour his attitudes in later life, so do his early
play experiences, particularly his sense of fun.

All the play ideas in this book have been checked for
safety by members of the staff of The Boston Children's
Hospital. In the hospital, we have a celebrated collection of objects that were removed from the stomachs
or throats of small children, including safety pins, buttons, nails, hatpins, peanuts, cup hooks—and a collection of political campaign buttons from Roosevelt to
Johnson. Our doctors have kept accidents very much
in mind while checking over the lists of play materials.

The 'safest' home, however, has potential hazards
and cannot be made truly safe even if it were desirable
to make it so. As children grow, they must learn
gradually to live with the hazards of everyday life. One
of the chief dangers in play is that a young child will
put things in his mouth. If it's sponge, it's all right. But,
if it's a tack or a bottle of nail polish, beware. In the
'three-, four- and five-year-olds' section we have used
beans, buttons and dry macaroni and other small objects which are dangerous to give children who still
chew everything. Most four-year-olds are no longer
interested in putting these things in their mouths and
can play with them safely. You will know whether or
not you feel your child is safe playing with these things.
If you're not sure, talk to your doctor about it.

CHOOSING WHAT TO DO WHEN

If the 'nothing to do' day comes when you're exhausted and short of ideas (or patience), consider your own capacities first. If you undertake a project

that seems burdensome to you, it's almost certain that your child won't enjoy it much either. You may not want to do anything at all; in that case you might make each child a nutritious peanut butter sandwich and turn on the TV. You can go to a nearby sofa and put your feet up. Forget about cooking supper. (But be sure your children are safe and you are where you can keep an eye on them.)

Useful as TV is, particularly around the supper hour, we don't recommend that you use it too much. Some children's TV programmes are very good but even so TV doesn't help a child to master his own skills.

There are many play ideas here on which your child, once you get him started, may play for a long time happily, all by himself. A three- or four-year-old can play safely in a nearby room with an oatmeal 'sandbox' or stringing used cotton reels. He won't need watching too closely. In the appendix under 'Good ideas when a mother is out of sorts,' you will find a chart of other safe ideas that don't require close supervision.

When choosing a play idea, consider how your child is feeling, too. Is he tired? Is he over-excited? Is he feeling floppy? Or is he just plain bored? You will find in the appendix another chart, 'Good ideas for a child who is out of sorts.' This has some suggestions for the sick or tired child as well as for the child who needs to let off steam. It is good to remember that when a child (or an adult) is sick or tired, he likes to return to the simpler play of an earlier age. Don't give him anything too exacting.

It also helps to follow the lead of nursery school teachers in alternating quiet and active play periods. After a stint with crayons, which require great concentration and control of the hand and eye muscles, let your child have a good fight with crumpled newspaper 'snowballs'. A potato race might follow some stitching on cardboard.

Many mothers have asked how to keep children from fighting or fussing during the last difficult hour before supper, without constantly relying on TV. Card or board games almost inevitably lead to squabbling at this hour, when the children are too tired to put up with rules and regulations. A few suggestions might be: clay or play dough, pasting, some picture books from the library which you have put aside for this hour, a bag of light small blocks plus a few plastic animals or dolls from Woolworth's. In any case, choose something quiet that a child can do by himself, without your help or the participation of his brothers and sisters. Friendly brotherly-sisterly participation rarely occurs in that hour before supper. But a little diversion at this crucial time of day can work miracles.

Although we have tried in this book to list play ideas according to chronological age, this has been a difficult job because no two children devolop exactly in step. Some toilet train themselves early, others later. Some two-year-olds have early hand-eye co-ordination, others are particularly attuned to music. Some stop putting things in their mouths at two, others not until five. You will know your own child and what he likes to do. If you see a game or toy listed for four-year-olds which might appeal to your two-year-old, or if he loves an activity in the baby section, let him enjoy it to his heart's content—if it's safe. But above all, don't worry if your three-year-old finds most of his fun in the toddler section. He'll learn soon enough. Pushing may only frustrate and discourage him.

The secret of successful play is choosing the activity which best suits your needs and those of your child at the moment. Playing with water in the kitchen sink, for instance, is a good activity when you must be working in the kitchen anyway. A visit to a food factory or to the florist might be fun on a day when you want to get out of the house and forget it.

On the other hand, if it's raining and your child has just fallen down and scraped his knee, and moreover has the sniffles and is at odds with his brothers and sisters, it may be that he doesn't want to do anything at all. He may just want to sit in your lap while you talk to him. Sometimes a song is good, too.

STARTING AND STOPPING

Almost every child needs help getting started—even if he's playing with something familiar that he can do by himself. After you have set out the materials, play with him for four or five minutes to help him get involved. Don't tower over him but sit down beside him or join him on the floor and show him how. Your own enthusiasm and fun will do a lot to interest him.

Before stopping play, give a child five or ten minutes warning to let him have time to finish what he's doing. If he's really interested and doesn't want to stop, be firm but talk about what he can do the next time he plays with these materials. It's important for play to end happily and for a child to realise that he can pick up at another time where he left off today.

And don't forget to praise a child for what he is able to do. The stagger on stilts, the lumpy piece of clay or the drippy mudpie are, in a very real sense, master-pieces. Children feel very proud to have their art work tacked up on the wall or shown to their fathers when they come home. Then the 'nothing to do' day suddenly turns into a day of triumph.

2

Babies

Although he sleeps a good part of each day, a baby will grow faster and change more during the first year of life than at any other age. His growth is fostered by his daily experiences with the world that immediately surrounds him. By touching things he learns where his body ends and the world begins. He learns to tell one sound from another by listening. He trains his eyes to focus by shifting them. Small objects help to teach him how to grasp and how to let go. At the centre of this world is his mother and without the loving attention of a single devoted person he would have grave difficulty growing at all. A mother and child's moments of play and pleasure together are the foundation of a baby's learning.

But no two babies are quite the same. Right from birth they seem to have distinct personalities and preferences. Some are cuddlers and love being held, patted and snuggled. Others are not so keen on cuddling and may even tense up or rear back if held closely. Some are restless and wakeful; others are placid and sleep a lot. Some love to be uncovered; others hate it. Some love sounds; others don't. But, in some way or other, all babies need lots of loving care. Look for the clues which indicate your baby's special needs and pleasures. It is his developing relationship with you that will encourage him to drink in new sights, sounds and sensations, to grow and learn new things.

The best time for play is when you both feel like it. It's hard for you to play if you're dead tired and it's hard for him if he's hungry or sleepy. But there is no sense to the old rule that a baby must be kept quiet and put to sleep after a feed, or that he shouldn't be bathed until he has digested his food. Some babies may spit up a little if handled roughly after a feed, but the value of the play far outweighs such a minor loss. In fact, the period surrounding both bathing and feeding times can be especially good play times.

Nor is it necessary to take a small baby outdoors every day. If you feel like going out and want to take the baby with you, by all means do, but he won't suffer by staying indoors.

The following play ideas are not all new. Many have been handed down by mothers through the centuries, but they are all supported by scientific research into how a baby learns. Pick out an activity that seems to suit you and your baby best at any particular moment. If your baby obviously doesn't enjoy it, try something else; the same criterion holds for you, as much as you can do what you both enjoy doing, when you both feel like it.

UNDER THREE MONTHS

Touching A baby's sense of touch is highly developed and he may learn more through touching and being touched than in any other way.

If your baby likes being held, there's nothing like the rocking chair. Motion and touch are combined plus comfort for mothers as well as babies. If you hold your baby on your shoulder as you rock, he may enjoy exploring your face with his fingers as he grows a little older. If you hold him in your arms or on your lap, he will grasp one of your fingers if you put it in his hand. (Babies can grasp at birth. This is an inborn reflex, not a conscious action on his part.)

When he's awake, take him with you from room to room (see looking chair, p. 32) so that he can see and hear you while you work. Some mothers carry their

babies around both inside the house and out in papoose rucksacks, or specially designed slings. So long as they are in a comfortable position, most babies like this closeness to their mothers and the motion of their bodies. Keep in touch with your baby through many senses—sight, sound and feel.

To quiet a crying baby, try wrapping him (fairly firmly) from the waist down in a napkin or blanket. Leave his arms free. The quieting effect of this kind of bundling is well known by people in other cultures who swaddle their babies a good deal of the time. They feel it gives the child a feeling of being held securely in his mother's arms. Another way to quiet a crying baby is a variation on swaddling; put your hand fairly firmly on his stomach or gently hold one of his arms or legs. This seems to have a quieting effect, especially if a baby is startled.

Listening From birth, babies are sensitive to sound and especially to high frequencies. As you bath or dress or feed your baby, sing, hum or whistle a tune you like. If you hit a few flat notes, your child will never notice. You may never have a more appreciative audience! For him, no disembodied voice coming from a machine can ever replace his own mother's singing.

Babies seem to be able to hear rather high-pitched sounds best and usually react more quickly to a woman's voice than to a man's. This may be the reason that 'baby talk' is usually high-pitched. However, a man's voice or a lower-pitched mixture of sounds such as those of an orchestra seem to be more soothing and more effective in lulling a child to sleep.

When you are not with your child, the gentle sound of a small clock ticking next to his cot or of a radio playing soft music may comfort him. A wind chime hung near his window where the breeze will catch it can be particularly soothing.

Looking A tiny baby spends most of his time lying down. His eyes are often focused upon the ceiling, the upper parts of the walls, and the sides of his cot. You can make these blank areas more interesting by hanging posters and pictures on the walls or fastening strips of coloured oilcloth on the inside of the cot. Bright colours that contrast with the background seem to be best. Strong reds and yellows seem to be particularly appealing.

Cot mobile Don't worry that your baby will grab any of these things and put them in his mouth. He won't do this until he's about three months old. But keep the trinkets high enough not to touch him if he turns over. Take a thin wooden rod such as a balloon stick or a thin bamboo plant stake and tie it across the width of the crib. With scotch tape or a bit of string, fasten onto it some of these things :

old costume jewellery
crumpled pieces of aluminium foil
coloured plastic spoons

bright paper cut into spirals, squares or circles
bits of bright cloth

Or, if you have a ceiling fixture, tie a string around it
and fasten a wire coat hanger to the bottom end of the
string. From the hanger, tie on different lengths of
string or thread and attach some of these articles to
the strings.

More sights   Babies often enjoy looking at lights. If
your baby seems fussy, put a lighted lamp (with a
shade) where he can look at it without hurting his
eyes. Or set a small coloured glass vase or drinking
glass on the window ledge for the sun to shine through.
Moving a fretful child to a different room will sometimes quiet him by giving him new things to look at.

The looking chair   Babies love to watch other children at play or their mothers busy with household
chores. It is well worth spending a few shillings for an
infant seat so that your baby can be part of the family
activity. It's easy to carry him from room to room in
this chair and he can also see what's going on without
straining his back or head. (Be sure the safety belt is
fastened so that he can't fall out.) If you put him on a
kitchen table, bed or sofa, be sure that he is in the
middle of it, in case he manages to tip the seat over.
This rarely happens even with an active infant, but
it makes sense to be careful.

A baby often likes to be in the centre of action. Try

strapping him into his infant seat and putting the seat in the middle of an empty playpen. The other children can then play outside the pen. The baby will be at their level to watch their movements and hear their chatter. He will also be somewhat protected from their attentions. But since they can still hurl toys at the baby or climb into the pen with him, be sure to keep a watchful eye.

Don't leave the baby alone in the room with other little children.

Bath time   Some young babies can be upset by baths. They don't seem to like that naked, exposed feeling and are sometimes startled by their own arm and leg movements. If your baby reacts this way, try wrapping him in a napkin or blanket before placing him in the water. Usually, after he is wet he will stop crying and you can remove the covering. (This is how women in India keep their babies happy in the bath.) Or, try gently holding his arm after he is undressed so that he doesn't thrash about so freely. This is often reassuring.

THREE TO SIX MONTHS

Cradle gym   As soon as a baby learns to reach and grasp (somewhere around four or five months), a mobile must be raised to a safe distance where he can't reach any fragile or possibly dangerous objects. Instead of a mobile, make a simple cradle gym with safe, smooth objects he can play with. Tie a length of heavy-guage elastic strapping across the cot, and attach short lengths of thinner elastic strips to it. Then, tie on two or three of these :

    an empty cotton reel
    smooth plastic spoons
    a rattle
    a large bell
    a smooth plastic bracelet
    other smooth-surfaced toys too large for him to
        swallow

Try this on the pram, too.

Squeeze toys   Pieces of worn towelling or oilcloth can be sewed together and stuffed with old nylon stockings. Babies this age prefer vivid colours of red, yellow, orange and purple to the more traditional pale pink and blue. Stuffed toys don't have to be teddy bears and dolls; a doughnut shape is easier for small hands to pick up.

Bounce chair   This is a good time to buy a bounce chair, sometimes called a Baby Bouncer—a chair with a plastic or canvas sling seat, which can be hung from its own frame or from above a door, with two holes in the front for the baby's legs. It allows the baby to sit up and bounce and, at the same time, protects the lower part of his back from strain.

Sometimes a baby of five or six months will bounce around too much and act a little groggy from so much motion. If your child seems floppy in his chair, try

tying the back of it to its metal stand on the floor. This stabilises the chair somewhat and keeps him from falling forward. It give him support similar to the infant seat.

Playpen toys Around four months, many babies start to spend time in a playplen. Some household items they enjoy holding or chewing are:

a smooth clothes-peg—the old-fashioned kind, not the springy, pinching type
a sponge

large empty reels—tie four or five on a string
a smooth plastic bracelet
a rattle
other smooth-surfaced toys too large for him to
  swallow

Games to play At about four or five months, most
babies like being carried to a mirror to see themselves
and their mothers or fathers. If you ask 'Who is it?' or
'What is that?', they are mystified and usually
delighted. This is the age, too, when babies begin to
learn to control parts of their bodies in simple movements, like nodding their heads or sticking out their
tongues. Try nodding your head and see if he imi-
tates you. Or make a clucking noise and see if he re-
sponds with one of his own. 'Oh' is a simple word he
may like to imitate.

Babies this age are also amused by hearing a sudden
change in pitch in someone's voice, from high to low

and back again. Try playing back and forth with your baby using these simple sounds and movements.

Bath time As he grows older, a baby is usually fascinated with water. When he enjoys sitting up in the bath, support his back and let him spend a few minutes splashing with his hand or kicking his feet. By this age, he probably won't want his bath wrapping any longer.

SIX TO NINE MONTHS

As a baby begins to sleep less, he begins to be able to play happily by himself for perhaps half an hour at a time. But he also wants to watch you while he plays.

This is the age for dropping and throwing things, for he is just learning how to let go of objects and he likes to experiment with his new knowledge. Spare yourself a lot of stooping and bending by tying toys to his bounce chair or pram. Put them on short strings or shoelaces and he can drop and then retrieve them by pulling up the string. Try :

a metal cup with handle

small metal pie tins (aluminium frozen-food and TV-dinner tins are ideal; make a hole for the string)

pot lids (tie the string to the handles)

fast dye ribbons

wooden spoons (to bang)

small tins (with a hole punched in end for stringing;

make sure the hole is too small for a tiny finger
and that edges are smooth)
small empty cardboard gift boxes
adhesive-bandage tins
old reels from cellophane or adhesive tape

In his playpen, he will push these things through the
slats or throw everything out on the floor. Tie them to
the playpen with short strings.

Bounce chair   If you've tied the bounce chair (see p.
34), your baby is probably now ready to bounce more
freely. Try removing the stabilising string and see if
he enjoys the more energetic movement.

Nesting toys   Around the age of seven months, a baby
begins to discover how to put one thing inside another.
He really isn't ready yet for square nesting toys, but a
variety of round empty metal tins will amuse him.
Start with a small frozen orange-juice size (be
sure there are no sharp edges from the tin opener)
and add other soup and vegetable tins of different
sizes.

Games   A baby this age loves to play with people he
knows. When he is feeling sociable, try some of the
time-honoured, well-loved nursery games. A six-
month-old child usually likes to be swung gently back
and forth. Hold him firmly with both your hands
under his armpits. Your child may also enjoy riding
cock-horse on someone's knee and being passed from

one well-loved person to the next. Some time around nine months he will be able to connect words with actions. He'll like 'Pat-a-cake', 'This little pig went to market' (wiggle his toes while you say it), and 'Peep-bo'. He'll usually respond to 'bye-bye' by waving his hand.

Feeding fun At his age, feeding time can become a wonderful play time. As your baby becomes more inter-ested in the spoon or cup, give him an extra one to bang with while you feed him with the other. As he gets more independent and less interested in your feeding him, give him some soft bits of bread or banana to pick up and put in his mouth by himself. While he's occupied with his own work, you can keep spoon-ing the messier foods into his mouth. In this way you encourage his growing ability to feed himself and keep alive his interest in food.

Water play When a baby learns to grasp and let go, he loves playing with a sponge or flannel in the bath. He can squeeze the sponge or suck it. It's all right for him to put it in his mouth. The bath water won't hurt him.

3
Toddlers and crawlers

Sometimes around eight months a baby starts to crawl and, soon after (between ten and twelve months), to pull himself to his feet by the side of his playpen. Before you know it, he has begun to toddle, and to toddle with amazing speed. Some babies crawl for a long time, others walk without doing much crawling first. Whether he's a crawler or a toddler, he'll gain experience quickly and then move about very fast.

Urged forward by his new sense of mobility, he is apt to become an undaunted explorer, with all the zeal but with none of the sense of danger of his grown-up counterpart. If not watched carefully, he'll run into a busy street, climb a ladder or try tasting the bleach underneath the kitchen sink.

THIS IS THE ACCIDENT AGE

It doesn't do much good to warn or scold. ('No! No!', 'Don't touch that!') or punish a child this age because he often can't understand the danger. Even if he does, his memory is short and he probably won't be able to remember your warning from one half hour to the next.

It's much safer and more relaxing to 'toddler proof' your house. Remove to a safe height all dangerous objects or things you treasure. Cover any unused electric sockets. Be sure all medicines are kept well out of his reach. Even if he crawls on to the bathroom basin (as many children do), he should not be able to reach medicine. Remove cleaning products—such as ammonia or furniture polish—from beneath the kitchen sink. Toddlers love to put everything in their mouths and are apt to eat or drink anything. They have been known to down half a tin of paraffin without minding the taste.

Outdoors, unless you have a safe and fenced-in garden, a toddler or crawler must be watched closely. Many mothers have been surprised by the quick-as-lightning speed of a child who, just a week or two before, sat placidly waving his rattle.

While requiring close supervision, a toddler needs lots of opportunities to try things on his own. He loves to 'do' and by 'doing' he builds up his confidence and his abilities.

With toys, his insatiable curiosity is a blessing. Although he's not likely to play with any one thing very long (and you shouldn't expect him to), he is pleased with anything new, from a rolled-up piece of paper to an empty jelly packet.

He loves hiding behind a chair or door and hearing some grown-up ask, 'Where's baby?' He likes you to

hand him something so that he can hand it right back to you. He loves it if his father swings him high in the air. He wants to be cuddled and sung to by his mother.

When a baby learns to walk, he suddenly has a new view of the world. He used to look up at the undersides of tables and chairs. People seemed as big as giants. Now he can see the tops of chairs and his view of grown-ups starts at their knees. Overnight his new perspective and his urge to explore make a playpen seem far too restrictive, and he may object (sometimes rather loudly) to being left to play in it.

On the other hand, you may have other things to do and don't want to keep running after him. At such times try using a 'furniture playpen' (see p. 44) and give him a few of the household items described on the following pages which are safe for him to play with without supervision. From time to time, join him in his space to start him off on a new game. Toddlers learn by imitation and it is usually necessary to engage their interest in a new activity by doing it with them for a few minutes first.

A FURNITURE PLAYPEN WITH SIMPLE TOYS

To make a furniture playpen, section off a fair-sized space in the corner of a room (away from electric points), with sofa and chairs and a suitcase or two. If your child can see you, he should be happier here than in a playpen. And this will save you running after him and worrying about what he's up to.

In his playpen (or elsewhere) see how he likes to play with some of these toys :

    wooden spoons
    nesting tins
    small metal pie tins
    squeeze toys

A waste paper basket of discarded letters   He will be engrossed for a long time pulling the stuff out. You'll have to put it back in again! (Be sure there is nothing harmful such as paper clips or glass in the basket.)

Line up old-fashioned clothes-pegs along the edge of a deep cake tin. After you have set them up, show him how to pull them off and drop them into the tin.

The game is even more fun if you line them up all over again.

Pots and Lids   Lots of noise, but lots of fun, too! For variety, hide some safe object like an orange juice tin in a pot and let the toddler find it by 'surprise' when he takes the lid off.

Metal Coffee Percolator   A toddler will love its various parts, fitting them together and then taking them apart again. For safety, remove the glass piece from the lid if it has one.

Large Scraps of Brightly Coloured Silk Ribbon, Velvet or Synthetic Fur Fabrics   are fun to feel and chew. Tie some of these to his playpen or pram. Be sure they are made of colour-fast materials.

Empty Gift boxes, Jar lids, Soap wrapping   intrigue a one-year-old more than a bought toy.

Mailbox   Cut a large round hole in the lid of a shoe box or cylindrical cardboard box. Show him how to drop used cotton reels or small blocks into it and dump them out again by taking off the lid.

Scribbling   Give him a large sheet of brown wrapping paper or a newspaper. Or take a large paper bag, tear it open so that it's flat, and tape the ends down to the floor or table so that it won't slide. Then hand a toddler two or three sturdy crayons and show him how to scribble. (Let him work on a surface which won't be damaged by crayon marks.)

PULL TOYS

A toddler likes to pull practically anything attached to the end of a string or rope. Choose something that doesn't weigh very much so that it won't bang the furniture. It shouldn't be able to splinter or crack either, since it might hurt the child. The most successful kind of pull toy should produce some sound when it is dragged around. So look through the house for articles which are lightweight, unbreakable, and not *too* noisy (for your own sake). Some good pull toys are :

an old metal measuring cup
old bracelets (wooden, heavy plastic or metal)
empty reels (thread, typewriter or film)
toilet paper or towel tubes
pine cones
old stuffed animals

small boxes
hair rollers
wooden spoons
metal jar caps (punch a tiny hole through the centre
   of the lid with a nail)

You can put two or three of these on the same string. Be sure to knot each object a few inches apart.

To make a *train,* attach several cartons or small boxes. To make a *centipede,* alternate metal jar caps and empty reels. Hair rollers strung end to end would make a marvellous worm.

Run a string through a carton from the lid to the bottom and secure it with a knot so it can be pulled around. Put in a handful of dry macaroni and tape the top on securely. This will make a lively noise when a child pulls or shakes it.

Empty shoe boxes   strung together with strong string, make trains, cars, boats.

KITCHEN PLAY

After a baby passes his first birthday, the kitchen becomes a more and more fascinating world, but he must be watched with an eagle eye to see that he doesn't get into the wrong places. The kitchen can be the most dangerous room in the house. For safety and long-time entertainment, you might try :

The reserved kitchen drawer   Set aside a low drawer, or shelf, and fill it with old pots and pans, pie plates, covers, empty tins, a percolator, teaspoons, and wooden spoons. If you can't spare an extra shelf or drawer, use a cardboard carton. While you are working in the kitchen, your child has his special drawer (or carton) with his own cooking toys.

CLIMBING AND CRAWLING

A table leaf and cardboard cartons   Support both ends of a table leaf or small wood plank with two small cartons or some large telephone books to raise it about eight inches off the floor. A small child will like crawling over his bridge.

Big grocery cartons   Cut out both ends of two or three cartons. Turn them over and line them up, and he has a tunnel.

Throw *a blanket* over a small table (a card table is ideal) and tie it on with a circle of rope. This makes a wonderful house and a good place to play peep-bo. Children like to play under tables or behind a sofa or big chair.

WATER GAMES, INDOORS AND OUT

Outdoors   If you're lucky enough to have a garden, even if it's only a bare patch of earth, you have what

your toddler enjoys playing with the most—earth, sand and water. An old tyre makes a good sandbox but it isn't necessary to have any box at all. Most one-year-olds ignore the box anyway, and dump and strew the sand everywhere.

Just a small pile of sand (of the coarsest, cheapest kind), some loose gravel and a pile of earth will keep a child happy for a long, long time. Give him a stick or spoon to dig with and a pan or small bucket of water. Bought sand-play tools don't work as well as big metal or wooden spoons. Large plastic bleach or starch containers with their tops cut off are ideal containers. An old sieve, colander or strainer from your kitchen is fine for sifting.

A toddler spends so much of his day being washed and changed that he usually loves having one spot where he can be as messy as he wants. For the garden, dress him in old things you don't care about, and then he can stir, dip and splash as much as he likes.

Indoors   Water is one of the most wonderful playthings a child can have. It has one major disadvantage for mothers, however. It is wet. The most convenient arrangement for water play indoors is to put your child into a dry bathtub in old clothes (or naked, if it's warm enough) and give him a pan of water. (Or, if it's easier for you, just draw a shallow bath.) There he can splash to his heart's content while you clean the bathroom or set your hair. (Be sure to stay in the bathroom with him.)

Give him some empty reels and small pieces of wood. He can make the reels 'ride' on wood 'boats'. Tightly capped, empty plastic bottles also float and are fun. So are soft soap flakes (and perhaps some water softener) for billows of bubbles. A laundry sprinker is good for squeezing and squirting.

MUSIC AND DANCING

Some children love music, others aren't so keen. But, for those who do, music—quiet or active—can be wonderfully restorative. Highly active or high-strung children often drift off to sleep more easily when listening to a lullaby or even more rhythmic music like jazz and rock 'n' roll. Don't overlook classical music.

For an 'activity' record, folksongs send toddlers happily bobbing around the room in time to the music. Many children fall in love with nursery rhymes at this age and continue to cherish them for years.

In the 'Children's Records' section (pp. 171–181) there is a list of folksongs, nursery rhymes set to music, and classical music. You will also find a list of books (p. 157) filled with songs that children have loved for generations. See if your local library has copies of either the songbooks or the records.

RHYMES AND READING

Even without music, babies this age like little rhymes and rhythms—like 'Pat-a-cake' or 'Jack-be-nimble'. They like to associate words with movements. If it's something you would do naturally, try reciting some nursery rhymes when you take him for a walk, change his napkin or put him in the playpen. Although a baby can't carry on a conversation, he loves the rhythm of someone else's words.

A good book can often capture the imagination of a child for a long time—sometimes from babyhood to school days. This is because children love familiar things, so that the same book can be used in a variety of ways. Where a one-year-old may enjoy hearing you read aloud to him, a fifteen-month-old child, who can sit comfortably in your lap, may like to do his own reading by naming the pictures. It's fun for him to be able to point to the objects he knows and tell you what they are—'dog', 'ball', 'tree', 'Daddy', 'house'.

In choosing a book for a toddler, it's a good idea to find one with very bright colours, even if they seem garish to you. This is because his eyes are not yet tuned to subtle hues or pastel shades, like pale pink, blue or yellow.

You can also make a fine book for a toddler yourself. Try:

Picture cards (without words) Cut cardboard into 5-inch by 8-inch cards and paste on each one a large, brightly coloured picture of something familiar, like a truck or cat or dog. The more realistic and sharply defined the picture, the better. The 5-inch by 8-inch card is just the right size for an eighteen-month-old child to hold and focus his eyes upon. He may talk to himself about each picture, repeating the word over and over.

On the other hand, he may not be at all interested in being read aloud to or in looking at pictures. Don't press him or he may take an active dislike to the whole business. He'll take to books soon enough. Try again in a few months' time.

4

For all ages:
a surprise and comfort bag

There are always those special occasions—the long
waits at the dentist's or sick in bed at home—when a
child must amuse himself quietly. These can be restless times for both mother and child. A 'surprise and
comfort bag', filled with new toys and hidden away for
special occasions, can often save the day. You will find
it useful for:

Trips to the doctor or dentist or hospital which sometimes involve long, boring periods of waiting
without play materials in the waiting room.
Trips to the beauty parlour, airport, or railway station when you must take your small child with
you.
Aeroplane, train or long car trips.
Trips to Grandmother's or to other households
where there are no other young children and few
toys around.
Sickbed days, when the surprise bag can be hung
over your child's bedpost or pinned to the sheets
at the side of the bed within easy reach.

To make a surprise and comfort bag   A paper shopping bag is ideal. Write your child's name on the outside with a marking pencil and then varnish the bag inside and out to make it waterproof and more durable. Or, use an airline bag or a plastic-coated shopping bag. Manila envelopes of various sizes may be stapled to the inside of the bag to keep the contents from becoming a jumble. Into one of these, stick a few paper towels or wash 'n' dry packets. They'll be useful for sticky faces and fingers.

It's best to have a special bag for each child.

What to put in Keep the surprise bag filled and ready
for service. You may want it in a hurry. It isn't necessary to buy anything; if your child hasn't seen an old
toy for a while, it will seem new to him. An old handbag filled with junk is fun, and so are sheets of unused
Christmas seals to stick on blank paper. A half-used
roll of scotch tape and some scraps of coloured construction paper and scissors can often occupy a child
for a long time, or an old pack of playing cards to sort.
What you keep in the bag obviously depends on your
child's age and his special interest. It is best, however,
to avoid noisy toys or things that roll away or which
might annoy other people. Dry finger foods like cereal
or raisins are good, but chocolate smears and soft
fruits get squashed. When you are shopping, keep
an eye open for little surprises that you can add to the
bag.

Some good things for the surprise bag:

playing cards for sorting and building
bean bag
flannel board and scraps of flannel
wooden boxes with lids, and something inside
    (empty walnut shells, for instance)
pipe cleaners
felt pens (washable)
thick crayons and pad of paper
blunt scissors
scotch tape

magnet
miniature doll family
old handbag with old keys, costume jewelry, hand-
    kerchief, etc.
sewing cards and wool (unsafe for travel)
magnifying glass
small animals and cars
pick-up sticks (unsafe for travel)
gummed labels, stamps and paper shapes, stars,
    moon, etc.
coloured paper
magic slate
colouring book
doctor or nurse kit
small boxes of raisins and dry cereal

'Comfort toys'   If you are going out, be sure to slip in
one or two of your child's favourite and familiar toys
just before you leave. At each age, a child will cling to
some toys which he especially cherishes—a teddy bear,
an old blanket. In a strange or unsettling circumstance,
these familiar things are especially comforting for they
are the child's link with home. These are the 'comfort
toys'.

The surprise bag at home   If your child is sad or
seems 'at a loose end' pick out one toy that might seem
new and special. This often saves a blue day. Or, if you
are leaving him with a new baby sitter, let him close his
eyes and dip into the bag for a 'surprise'. If he is sick

in bed, pin the whole bag to the side of the bed but keep only a few toys in it at a time. You can exchange toys as the day goes on, thus producing new 'surprises' thoughout the day.

5

Two- and three-year-olds

The child from two to three loves familiar old toys. He usually has a ragged piece of blanket or an old stuffed toy he takes everywhere with him. He doesn't really play with other children yet; he may hug or poke or else totally ignore them. He isn't a sharer of toys, for he wants to keep his own special treasures to himself. Let him do this and have plenty on hand for the other children. He'll get more sociable when he's three or older.

All young children differ from one another in developing their muscular skill and social abilities. Some become skilful with their hands easily; others may instead be training their ears or eyes. For this reason, we have called this chapter 'Two- and three-year-olds' and the next chapter, 'Three-, four- and five-year-olds'. Most of the ideas in the next section are for older three-year-olds, but your child may have developed a special ability in hand-eye co-ordination, for instance, and might want to try something in the next section. Just be sure it's safe. Remember, too, that when they are tired or sick, children prefer the simpler play of earlier ages.

Many a two-year-old's favourite word is 'no'. He's just beginning to assert himself and this means testing his will and yours. It can be exasperating, but if he weren't negative at times, he wouldn't be developing.

Often, if you don't make an issue of it, you can simply ignore his protest. Sometimes he really means 'no'. Then it's best to distract him. Fortunately, he can be distracted quite easily, especially if you let him make his own choices. If he is feeling very negative it often works better to show him two objects and when he reaches for one, rapidly remove the other. If you ask him, 'Do you want the blue crayon or the purple one?' he may get completely hung-up over the choice.

This is the age, too, when a child is apt to be pre-occupied with his bowel movements. That is one reason why a two-year-old finds wet and gooey substances so fascinating. With other toys, his attention span is very fleeting, but if you give him a pan of water and some sand or mud, he'll probably play for a long time.

Play ideas the two-year-old still enjoys:

his own picture book without words
floating bath toys
squeeze toys
reserved kitchen drawer
table leaves and cardboard cartons
table-house

WATER PLAY

If you're working in the kitchen, let your child stand
on a sturdy chair and use a bowl in the sink. Spread
newspapers on the floor to soak up the drippings and
protect his clothes with a plastic apron. (Make a
poncho by cutting a round hole in the middle of an old
plastic cot sheet or tablecloth and pull it over the
child's head.) Keep this home-made poncho in place
by tying a heavy string around his waist. Or, all
else failing, let him wear his bathing suit on a hot day.

Mothers aren't always keen about letting their
children play with water in the house except in the
kitchen or bath. But, if you must be busy in some
other room and your child wants to join you, you can

waterproof any small area by spreading an old shower curtain or plastic tablecloth on the floor and covering it with a thick layer of newspaper. Set a small bowl half full of warm water in the middle.

For the kitchen sink or the living room bowl, here is a fine collection of toys:

> funnel
> measuring spoons and cups
> handkerchiefs or doll clothes (to wash)
> cake tins
> juice tins
> sieve
> small plastic jug
> plastic baster or laundry dampener
> plastic squeeze bottle (empty)
> piece of floating soap
> sponge
> plastic ice-cream containers

For more fun, add a few drops of food colouring and some liquid detergent to the water. Let him stir them in.

Soap bubbles Give your child a plastic drinking straw and a cup (or empty juice tin) filled with soap flakes and water. Children of two and a half and older can learn to blow, not suck, if you show them how. Since the cup is bound to over-flow, it is best to use a tray under it. To make bubbles tough enough to float in the air without breaking, add a tiny bit of cooking oil to the soap-and-water mixture. The bathtub and outdoors are good places for soap bubbles.

CLAY PLAY

Children between two and three love to play with something they can pound and squeeze, break apart and put together again. Tearing and pounding give them an opportunity to express feelings they are not yet able to put into words. A fretful child will often be much calmer and happier after a good pounding session with clay.

All the ingredients for clay are right in your kitchen.

Play dough

1 cup salt
1½ cups flour
½ cup water
2 tablespoons oil
a few drops of food colouring (optional)

This dough lasts for weeks if you store it in the refrigerator in a plastic bag or a covered jar. Children can pull and pound it, and then it can be collected and put away for another day, or they can make 'things' and leave them out to dry and harden. (Small children may put this dough in their mouths. It won't taste good, but it won't hurt them.) Let your child sit at the kitchen table or on the floor, using a baking sheet for a working space. Dust his hands with a little flour so that the dough won't stick to his fingers. He may just want to pound and squash the dough with his hands. Or he might have fun with :

a rolling pin
biscuit cutters
blunt knives, forks, and spoons

PASTING

Children usually don't paste very well until they are three or older, but younger ones love to mess with it. Some mothers give their two-year-olds a pat of vaseline or cold cream to smear over a baking sheet and they have a fine time making swirly patterns. This may seem a strange idea, but, actually the vaseline or cream is easier to wash off than mud; and it helps some small children who have a great urge to be messy become more co-operative. If they put a little in their mouths, it won't hurt them. (Naturally, you will have to watch and see that they don't start smearing the stuff on the walls and furniture.)

Or try this recipe for home-made no-cook paste :

a handful of flour
add water (a little at a time) until gooey (it should
   be quite thick, so it won't run all over the paper)
add a pinch of salt

This no-cook paste is not so sticky as boiled paste (p. 86), but if you haven't the time or the facilities to cook, this paste holds scraps of paper together pretty well. Although it doesn't taste delicious, it won't hurt

a child if he puts some in his mouth. Your child may be happiest just smearing this paste on a baking sheet. Or he may like to try sticking scraps of paper together. Any scraps will do. They should be about the size of Christmas cards.

PAINTING

The floor is a good place for the two-year-old painter. The colours won't run and drip as much as they do on an easel or a table. Start off with a big supply of large pieces of paper and a big paint brush, at least three quarters of an inch wide at the bottom. A hardware paintbrush lasts longer and costs less than an artist's paintbrush. For paint and water containers, use a tin or fairly flat, wide plastic bowl.

A child of this age does better with just one colour. Any kind or colour of paper is fine. Try:

newspaper (a two-year-old will paint all over the
print without noticing it)

large paper bags cut in half

white butcher's paper (wrappings off your meat
packages)

used gift-wrapping paper

brown wrapping paper

shelf paper

shirt cardboards

Use poster paints. The powder is less expensive and
lasts longer, and you need mix only a little at a time.

A two-year-old's pictures will consist of a few wavy
lines, or dots, or a single blob of colour. He tends to
discard sheet after sheet with only a line or two on it,
so give him the cheapest paper you can find. Don't ask
him what his picture is supposed to be; it isn't supposed
to be anything. He's learning that he can make
his 'mark' and that's enough. You may want to save
some of his efforts, but he doesn't care a hoot about
them. It's the doing that matters.

Finger-painting (See p. 82)

OTHER HAND PLAY

Puzzles which are simple, big and brightly coloured
are loved by two-year-olds. You can make them at
home quite easily. Try one of these:

Pie puzzle Take a piece of thick cardboard, such as
the side of a carton, and draw a large circle on it by

outlining the bottom of a cooking pot; cut out the circle and then, with a pencil and ruler, divide it into fourths. Colour each segment a different colour with crayons or poster paint.

Moon puzzle Make another large circle and draw a moon three quarters full. Cut the circle into two or three arc-shaped pieces and paint each a different colour.

Triangle puzzle Make a triangle with four-inch sides. To do this, draw a horizontal line four inches long. At the midpoint of the horizontal line, draw another line perpendicular to the first. Then draw lines four inches long (with a ruler) from each end of the horizontal line to the vertical one. (They should meet.) Cut out the triangle. Then cut the triangle in half along the vertical line. Paint or crayon the two parts.

House or aeroplane puzzles Cut out of a magazine a large and colourful picture of an aeroplane, a house, or a boat. Glue it to a piece of cardboard and cut the cardboard to fit it. (Cardboard that comes in shirts is good; so is the backing on large pads of paper.) Then cut the house, boat or aeroplane into two or three unequal pieces.

Feltboard Paste a colourful piece of felt on a piece of heavy cardboard. Cut shapes out of scraps of felt (from old hats), flannel, or velveteen. If you're feeling artistic, you can make animal or people shapes (if you can't draw, trace them) but odd shapes do every bit as well. Show your child how to put the shapes on the felt so that they will stick. This is fine for unsupervised play and creates no mess to clean up.

Oatmeal sandbox   You can have a small sandpile in your kitchen simply by putting fine oatmeal into a big metal baking pan. If your child puts some meal in his mouth, it won't hurt him. Put the pan on the kitchen table, on newspapers on the floor, or on the back steps. Here are some good things to play with in an oatmeal 'sandpile'.

   funnel
   cake tin
   sieve
   tablespoon
   measuring cup and spoons
   small toy cars and trucks
   juice tins (with smooth edges)
   empty cottage-cheese or half-pint cream cartons

Reel stringing   A child of almost three may have enough control of his finger muscles to try reel stringing. Empty wooden reels of thread painted bright colours are as much fun as real beads, and a lot easier. Give him a long string with the ends pointed and stiffened with adhesive or plastic tape. A very long shoe lace is ideal. Each reel sliding on the string will represent a lot of hard concentration, so don't push him if he isn't yet ready for this exacting kind of hand-craft.

CLIMBING AND CRAWLING

Climbing helps the two-year-old to develop the large muscles of his arms, legs and torso and he is astonishingly sure-footed. If you live in the country or suburbs, you may be able to find an *old wooden ladder* and get someone to saw off a section of it, about three or four

rungs (no higher). This can be leaned against a wall or house for climbing indoors or outdoors. You can also make a good bridge by supporting a *large wooden plank* with a couple of *large and sturdy toy building blocks* (just a few inches off the floor or ground). Crawling over this plank bridge helps to develop your child's sense of balance.

Planks Your timber yard may give away small odds and ends of planks. They will be used endlessly if they are light and small enough for a small child to lug around. Sand them down so that there are no splinters.

GOING PLACES

A two-year-old enjoys an outing most if the whole family goes along. The excursion should be kept short and simple, since his endurance is limited. A walk to feed the pigeons, to see the ducks in spring, or to visit the local pet shop is enough. If you take him to the zoo, bring his push chair along and make the visit very brief.

READING ALOUD

Between two and three, a child sometimes becomes fascinated by one particular book or record and wants to hear it over and over again. On some days he may listen as long as patience holds out. Be careful not to change a word or skip a line. On other days, he may not be interested at all.

He'll especially enjoy simple stories like *Goodnight Moon* with its many repetitions of words that rhyme.

Books that two-year-olds usually enjoy are listed in the 'Children's Books' section (p. 157) where a note is made of those titles particularly suitable for very young children but attention could perhaps be drawn to the two books by Norah Montgomerie, the Bod Books by Michael and Joanna Cole and *The Story of Ping* amongst others and of course, *The Story of Little Black Sambo* and *The Tale of Peter Rabbit*—early and lasting favourites with the young of all ages.

MUSIC AND DANCING

A two-year-old likes music with a definite beat and he 'listens' by moving and swaying his whole body. If he has trouble going to sleep at night, you might play him some of the selections from 'Music for Listening' (p. 180–1), or sing to him yourself. He'll usually want to hear that same song or record over and over again, just like a favourite book.

The song books listed on p. 170 are full of children's songs for singing or playing on the guitar or piano. You are still your child's favourite performer.

6

Three-, four- and five-year-olds

A three-year-old is a sociable type. He loves to play or work together with his parents, making them show him just how to do things. He is insatiably curious about the world around him and likes to try his hand at new enterprises.

As he grows older, about four or five, he begins to prefer to play with friends, often slightly older children who teach him more new tricks. He's very proud when he succeeds in hammering a nail into a piece of wood or in stringing beads on a shoelace. Be proud, too. These are real accomplishments. If he hasn't developed the necessary manual dexterity or interest yet, don't push him, but praise him for what he *can* do.

Between three and six there are tremendous swings back and forth between striving to be grown-up and wanting to return to the more comfortable life of babyhood. One day a child may want to conquer the whole world (and fully believe that he can!) and the next day he may want to cling and be cuddled. He's torn between his fantasy (and desire) to be big and the

terrible reality that he is still very small and needs his
parents very much. Support your child's efforts to move
forward by helping him master the things which he is
capable of doing. Gently distract him from taking on
projects that are too much for him to master and will,
therefore, make him feel frustrated and defeated.
When he's feeling in a clingy or ill mood, let him play
in the simpler ways of two-year-olds. The next day, or
the next week, he'll start out to conquer again.

A three-year-old's accomplishments are obviously
much cruder and more primitive than those of a four-
or five-year-old. But that doesn't lessen any of his
satisfaction in doing them. Also, a three-year-old will
need more help in setting up, beginning, and doing
than an older child does. If you enjoy participating and
lending a hand, many activities—the painting, clay,
pasting ones, especially—can be simplified for a three-
year-old.

Some of the activities in this section are dangerous
for younger children. So, if you have smaller children
as well, be sure they don't get into the older child's
playthings.

Some favourite activities carry over from earlier
years. These are still popular:

water (p. 63)—a four- or five-year-old loves whip-
    ping a handful of soapflakes into a high foam
    with an egg-beater.
oatmeal sandbox   (p. 70)
reserved kitchen drawer (p. 48)

BUILDING

From three to six, blocks are among the best toys a child can have. Wooden blocks are easily made by sawing 2-inch by 4-inch timber into lengths of three, six, twelve, and twenty-four inches. These should be sanded smooth to eliminate splinters. You can also use:

Full tins and grocery packets   You may think of these as things that belong on the shelf, but they can be wonderful toys. In fact, they make better building blocks than any you can buy in the shops. Use full tins

that aren't too large or heavy. At the first sign of wear, you can rescue the packets!

Shoe boxes and cigar boxes   If you tape on the lids they make fine blocks.

Clothes-pegs   The spring variety make fine construction tools for three-year-old and up. Just give him a batch and show him how to attach one onto another and you'll be surprised at the constructions that result.

TEARING, RIPPING AND PUNCHING

Before they learn to make things (and after that, too) children love just to rip and tear. Keep a stack of old magazines and newspapers on hand as his 'special pile' for 'his work'. Sit down beside the pile and show him how to tear. Then show him how to poke holes with the handle end of a wooden spoon. He'll have a great time making a snowstorm of newsprint all around him. Afterwards, it can be scooped up in a matter of seconds. Tearing and poking are good ways for a child to learn to use the small muscles of his hands, and also provide a safe outlet for aggressive feelings.

Old sheets   Let the children tear up an old sheet. They love to rip up cloth! Little boys especially feel strong when they succeed in demolishing a good-sized piece. The pieces make good bandages for make-believe wounds. You can keep a carton or drawer of worn-out linens 'just for play'. (Don't worry about starting 'bad habits'. If you give him his special sheet or pillowcase to tear, he won't go around ripping up other things. If you let him vent his energies and strength on this sort of harmless action, he's apt to be less destructive elsewhere.)

Hole punch This is a tool which fascinates a child. Just let him punch away on a newspaper. If he uses white waxed paper, save the little punched-out discs. They can be put in a jar full of water and, after you fasten the lid on tightly, he can shake the jar and make a 'snowstorm'.

Tear a mural Give your child a variety of textures of paper (smooth and bumpy, heavy and tissue-thin) of different colours and perhaps some patterned paper. Then ask, 'Can you tear a *tiny* shape?' 'A great big *enormous* shape?' 'How about a *wide* shape?' Then let him paste all the interesting ragged shapes on a long piece of paper for a great big, colourful mural. If you have an empty wall, tack the mural on the wall for all to see.

PAINTING, DRAWING AND COLOURING

Children delight in making pictures, even if they are just scribbles on a big paper bag or sheet of newspaper. Colouring books are useful at times but children more often prefer to draw their pictures in their own way. He shouldn't be made to feel his picture must look like 'something' to grown-ups. To him, it *is* 'something' and his imagination is hard at work.

A three-year-old can draw simple shapes like circles or crosses and can also experiment with different strokes. He is beginning to notice the results of his efforts and, in this respect, your praise and encouragement are important. A child puts on paper what he

thinks and feels, not what actually exists in the real world. Appreciate his efforts, and let him know that you are accepting him and his unique view of life. If you ask, 'What is it?' and he doesn't know, don't press him for an answer. Better not say, 'Here, let me help,' for he would much rather do it alone.

A three-year-old needs a separate big brush for each paint pot and he can learn to use the right brush for the right colour. He can also wash his brushes when he's finished and put them away, if you show him how. He's happy to paint his pictures sitting either on the floor or at a table.

It is usually not until after his fourth birthday that a child produces paintings which adults can recognise as pictures. By this age he has a pretty clear idea of what he is trying to draw. If some of the proportions or colours strike you as rather strange, don't let the child know it. If you say, 'I like the way you gave that dog those lovely orange ears,' he'll be happier. 'Whoever heard of a dog with orange ears?' fills a child with doubt and inhibits his next efforts.

It helps if you hang up many of the pictures painted by the child between three and six. Tack them up on walls or hang them by clothes-pegs from a line hung across the room. They'll be highly decorative.

Paper :

    printers' remnants (often high-quality paper in interesting textures which the printer is glad to give away)

    newsprint paper (largest and cheapest paper available in art shops)

    large paper bags cut in half (all colours; if patterned or printed on, use the other side).

    white butcher's paper (great for finger-painting); save these from your meat purchases or ask a nearby butcher if he can spare a little

wallpaper books (use the blank sides for painting and drawing; the patterned sides may be used for pasting. At certain times of the year, wallpaper dealers will give you these books free, because they go out-of-date.)

brown wrapping paper

shelf paper

shirt cardboards

paper plates

wax paper (This versatile art material is marvellous for tracing, or older children can scratch pictures on it with a toothpick. They can also put wax paper over the funnies and rub the surface with a spoon. The colour will come off on the wax paper, making a reverse picture.)

carbon paper (Staple two pieces of paper together with carbon paper in between and let your child draw with a pencil or crayon. His picture will appear on the second sheet, too. He'll love this magic.)

PAINT

Flour and water finger-paint Children love to fingerpaint and now and then it's really worth the mess (and it *will* be a mess). Mix flour and salt with a little water to make a paste the consistency of thick gravy. Sprinkle in a little food colouring. Cover the children's clothes with aprons or old shirts and let them paint with their hands directly on the kitchen table. Put spoonfuls of the paint on the table, and let them slide their hands in it. As they work, sprinkle in a little more food colouring to change the colour. If you want to save a picture, press shelf paper over the tabletop art work and the paint will stick to it. Have a sponge handy to mop up. You can let them finger-paint on the kitchen linoleum floor. The paste isn't tasty but it won't hurt them to put some in their mouths. Food colouring won't stain and you can mop it right off.

Shaving-cream finger-paint Buy a tube of shaving cream and let him use it on the kitchen table. The smooth texture will delight your child. Some coloured powder paint sprinkled here and there will sustain his interest. When the cream begins to dry, a few drops of water or more shaving cream can be added. Here the process is more important than the product. When finished, the cream wipes off easily with a dry towel and is less messy to clean up than finger-paint. This is good for two-year-olds, too. It won't hurt them to put some in their mouths.

Liquid-starch brush paint[1] Liquid starch makes elegant paint. Put a cup of it on the table, give your child a pastry brush, or better still, a hardware paintbrush from your husband's supply, and some dark paper (a cup-up paper bag will do, but dark-coloured paper is better). The starch paint will dry on the paper just

---

[1] Unsafe for a child who still puts things in his mouth.

as poster paint does. If you want to use white paper, add a little food colouring to the liquid starch. If you're out of starch try :

Soap-flake paint Just mix a little water with soap flakes to make a paste and add food colouring if you wish. This is pretty good paint, but not as effective as starch.

If you don't want to bother making paint, get poster paint. Buy the powder, not the liquid; it's cheaper and you can mix a little at a time with water in baby food jars. Two or three different colours are plenty.

Store home-made paints in baby food jars

To dry finished paintings, drape them over a clothes rack or hang them outdoors on a line with clothes-pegs.

PENS, CRAYONS AND CHALK

Ball-point pen Children love to draw with Mummy or Daddy's ball-point pen; they feel very grown-up indeed.

Marking pencil A felt-tipped marking pencil is a wonderful drawing toy for a child. Put down some newspaper and give him a big cardboard box to draw on. Keep your child in the same room with you, or he's apt to wander out of sight and begin decorating the furniture and walls! One mother let her children mark hair on their chests to play Tarzan. It took two weeks to wash it out! Get the washable marking pencils. They're easier on mothers.

Crayons, more than any other plaything, can be a mother's greatest friend. Like blocks, crayons go on for years but, unlike blocks, they can be tucked into a small bag to be used in doctors' waiting rooms, in the car, or on visits to Granny. For these early ages, be sure to get the large fat crayons that don't break under heavy pressure from little fingers. Four or five different coloured crayons are enough.

Chalk   Big fat pieces of soft chalk in vibrant colours encourage free-flowing pictures. The colours mix together easily, making beautiful combinations. (But if your child wants to keep putting one on top of the other until it's all muddy grey, that teaches him about colours, too.) Try wetting paper bags and letting him draw on them. The chalk becomes fluorescent.

PRINTING[1]

Pour a little poster paint or home-made paint (pp. 82–84) into a shallow pan and put a few paper towels on the bottom to make a stamping pad. Give your child a few big sheets of white paper (shelf paper is good) or cloth (old sheets are great). Cut a potato in half, or a green pepper, or cucumber, and show him how to rub the vegetable slice over the paint-soaked towels and then print it onto the paper or sheet.

[1] Might be a little too difficult for three-year-olds.

(A child may drag the slice back and forth over the paper rather than making one firm imprint. That takes practice and he'll learn in time; meanwhile, he's having just as much fun.)

These things also make fine printing forms:

keys[1]
hair rollers
sponges
pencils
leaves
half an orange or lemon
a wire whisk
a small wooden spoon

You can use anything which makes an interesting outline and which won't be hurt by the paint. If he's really having fun, you might let him decorate a whole roll of white shelf paper or paper towels.

PASTING

Children love making three-dimensional pictures they can feel. You can use the no-cook flour-and-water paste on p. 66. If you use quite a lot of salt, it will crystallise and sparkle when it hardens.

Or you can cook this *home-made 'boiled' paste*:

½ cup of flour
add cold water until it is thick as cream
simmer and stir on stove for five minutes

[1] Watch out for the keys if your child still puts things in his mouth.

add a few drops of wintergreen to give it a pleasant
    smell

add a few drops of food colouring to make it pretty

store in refrigerator in air-tight jar when not in use
    (Boiled paste lasts longer and sticks better than
    no-cook paste. No harm done if a child tastes this
    paste.)

Collage is the French name for artistic composition
that's pasted together. Give your child a paper bag
(cut in half and pressed flat) and let him paste on
some :

biscuits
raisins
dry puffed cereals
coloured paper scraps
fluffy cotton wool
scraps of coloured cloth

Then let him add some lines and colour with
crayons, instant markers, or chalk. (All these materials
are safe for three-year-olds who are still putting things
in their mouths; none will stick in the throat.)

Four- and five-year-olds may like to make more
elaborate collages of eggshells, wood, shells and buttons
using an adhesive like Bostik.

Children of four and older can handle blunt-tipped
scissors fairly well and most have stopped putting things
into their mouths. (If there is any danger of this, don't
let them use the materials below.) Here are just a few
good collage materials for older children :

dried-up flowers
dry macaroni
large buttons
small shells
leaves
dried beans
seeds
bits of wood
eggshells

You will think of others.

Paper chains   Cut a coloured magazine picture into one-inch strips. Show your child how to make a circle of one strip, and paste or scotch-tape the ends to each other. Then he can put a second piece through the first circle and glue it together and so on, until he has made a paper chain. These bright chains stretch as long as your child's patience. For Christmas tree decorations, use glossy gift-wrapping paper.

Cellophane tape and masking tape Children love tearing tape off the roll and sticking it to itself or to anything. If they have trouble handling the sticky stuff, try cutting off a number of small pieces and attaching them to a table edge to be used as needed.

Paper plates Children can decorate plates for special holiday parties (with paints or crayons) or make them into funny hats by gluing on decorations and then tying under the chin with a piece of string. A five-year-old

may enjoy cutting out numbers from an old calendar and making a clock on a paper plate.

CLAY MODELLING

Usually by the time he is four, a child no longer wants just to squeeze and pull and pound a lump of clay. He still enjoys this, but he also wants to *make* something, a real object with a name, which he can save. So he moulds streams of snakes, round balls, snowmen, cakes, and dishes. He also likes to paint his creations. By the time he is five, the objects become even more realistic. He often makes separate arms, legs, and heads, and then joins them together to make an animal or a person. Four- and five-year-olds may model human figures with very large breasts and genitals, or with parts broken off or missing. At this age, children are fascinated by the difference between boys and girls. It's natural for them to wonder if perhaps parts of their bodies are detachable or could be cut or broken off. It helps ease such unspoken concerns to translate them into clay. Don't let any exaggerated creations worry you. They provide a good opportunity for you to talk a little about how boys and girls are made.

A good recipe for home-made clay :

> 1 cup of flour, 1 cup of salt, enough water to make a very stiff dough.

This home-made clay will harden and can be painted. However, it is extremely brittle when dry and breaks easily. If your child finds this upsetting, you will win his gratitude by buying a more durable modelling material. You can get pottery clay in toy and art shops for a few shillings whereas plasticine is expensive and too difficult for small hands to manage. This pottery clay will last indefinitely if you put it into a large pottery crock with a lid. Make a hole in the middle of the clay in the crock and fill it with water to keep the clay moist. Some pottery clays need to be baked in the oven and others harden into a stone-like finish without heat.

SEWING, PLAITING AND KNITTING

Doll's clothes without any sewing[1] A little girl can make dresses for her doll by taking a rectangle of cloth, cutting out a head hole (with blunt scissors) and tying it on the doll with a sash. A blouse can be made from a short rectangle; a dress, from a long one; a skirt, from just a length rolled around the doll's middle. Pieces of ribbon add a fashion touch.

Real sewing[2] The best way to get children started (boys love to sew, too!) is to give them sewing cards. Cut pieces of cardboard in 6-inch squares (covering them with brightly coloured paper, if you like), then punch holes about an inch apart around the edges. Show your child how to thread in and out of the holes with a shoelace or a string. (Stiffen the ends of a string by wrapping them with cellophane tape.)

If your child is really interested, give her (or him) a real needle and thread. Cut an 8-inch square piece of loosely knit material which a needle will go through easily. (Make her use a blunt darning or tapestry needle. Standard needles are too difficult for small children and also may cause accidents.)

A four- or five-year-old likes to sew just for the fun of sewing, without wanting to make anything you can recognise. It will become 'something' in his or her eyes, however. Some five-year-old girls become passionately interested in sewing and learn to make bags, crude pot

[1], [2] May be hard for three-year-olds.

holders, and doll's capes and skirts (with some guidance and help). They can also sew net into ballet skirts and can be trusted to use electric scissors without hurting themselves (if you stand by).

Plaiting[1]   Cut heavy wool scraps or old nylons into long, thin pieces. Fasten these to a doorknob and show your child how to plait. This is a fine occupation which can be dropped and taken up again, without having to be put away.

Knitting needles and string   Sometimes boys and girls who are nearly six can learn to knit with big wooden needles and string (which doesn't separate like wool). Maybe Grannie will pick up all the dropped stitches for them.

IDEAS FOR MOTHERS WHO LIKE TO SEW

Cloth book   Cut four or five pieces of plain coloured cloth (the sturdier the better, canvas is good) into 12-inch by 16-inch pieces. Lay them evenly on top of each other and sew a seam down the centre to bind them together. Your child can now decorate each page with crayons. When he is finished with his masterpiece, press each page with a warm iron (protect your iron and ironing board cover with two sheets of blotting paper on top of each page and another underneath). The crayon marks melt into the cloth and become permanent.

[1] May be hard for three-year-olds.

Rag doll On a piece of material, draw the doll's outline, then cut out two identical pieces and sew them together around the edges, leaving a small opening. Turn the doll cover inside out (so that the seams are inside) and then stuff it like a pillow with old nylons. After you have filled the body and arms and legs and closed up the opening, sew seams at tops of arms and legs, and you'll have a 'jointed' doll. With felt tip pen, draw a heart on the doll's chest with a message—'I love [your daughter's name]'.

SORTING

After three, a child loves to sort things. When other friends come to call, sorting will often keep two or three children busy and happy for twenty minutes or more. It helps to teach them to judge size and develops co-ordination between eyes and hands. An easy way to begin sorting is to let your child help you sort the laundry. Sorting isn't always simple for a three-year-old, so don't be surprised if your child finds it puzzling at first.

Buttons[1] If you have a big collection of all shapes and sizes of buttons, they have many play possibilities. Give each child an empty egg carton, and let him sort them according to size. Or he can drop them into empty salt cylinders. Make slits of different lengths in the lids of several boxes. If you show them how, they can also

[1] Button games are unsafe for a child who still puts things in his mouth.

use buttons to lay out twisting and intersecting road-ways on the rug, but this game takes 'billions of buttons'.

Cards　Several packs of old playing cards will also amuse a small group of children for quite a while. The younger children can sort the pack into hearts, diamonds, clubs and spades. The older children will want to sort them according to the numbers and pictures which are alike.

Other things to sort (if the children can be trusted not to put them in their mouths) include : lentils, beans, cloves, various kinds of macaroni, shells, coins and old beads.

[1] May be hard for three-year-olds.

STRINGING

Dry macaroni[1] Take some short pieces of macaroni (the kind with holes all the way through them), and string them like beads to make necklaces and bracelets. The best string for a young child is a shoelace (if you haven't an extra one, take one out of his shoe). If you use string, put cellophane tape around the tip to make it stiff. For gay colours, let your child paint the

[1] Unsafe for any child who still puts things in his mouth.

macaroni with food colouring and dry it before he strings it.

Pipe cleaners   These are marvellous playthings for almost any age from three to eighty-three. Just twisting them into shapes and attaching them to one another can create an assortment of creatures from elephants to dolls. Regular white pipe cleaners from the tobacco shop are fine, but you can get colourful pipe cleaners of varying thicknesses.

Straws and pipe cleaners   Cut the pipe cleaners into two-inch pieces. Show your child how to push a straw onto each end of the pipe cleaner. The pipe cleaner will act as a joint and can be bent in any direction you like. Keep adding more straws (any length you like) and pipe-cleaner joints until he has the 'thing' he wants. For variation: Make a hole in a small piece of coloured paper and push it on the pipe cleaner before you join it to the straws.

WILD CREATIONS

Most children of four and five, if given an assortment of materials and encouragement, love to make imaginative 'creations'. Try giving your child some paste or cellophane tape and a motley collection of pine cones, toothpicks, plastic containers, walnut shells, scraps of bright paper and cloth, pieces of cork or potato, old-fashioned clothes-pegs, bits of clay, straws, ribbon and pieces of polystyrene. (You'll think of even

better things.) Sometimes, he likes to make 'a creation'. At other times, he may prefer to make something specific, like a doll out of clothes-pegs, or a boat out of the walnut shells.

Plastic-carton animals[1]   The plastic cartons used in food stores make good skeletons for animals. A 'lion', for instance, can be made by drawing and colouring a lion's face on a stiff piece of paper, cutting it out, and gluing it against one side of the plastic container. Attach pipe cleaners for legs, and wool for a mane and a tail. It isn't necessary to cover the carton itself with anything. It can also be cut into different shapes with a pair of heavy scissors. Hung from a hanger, it becomes a mobile.

Clothes-peg dolls   Old-fashioned clothes-pegs make

[1] May be hard for three-year-olds.

good dolls. Let your child wrap bits of cloth around them for a dress or around the two prongs for pants. A ribbon or string makes a belt. What about hair? (Bits of wool, clay, paper.) Arms? (Straws, pipe cleaners.) Then show him how to draw the eyes, nose and mouth on the 'head' with a crayon or a ball-point pen.

Walnut-shell boats[1]   Empty walnut shells make fine boats. Use burned matches for masts and hold in place with play dough. Scraps of white cloth or paper can be the sails. These boats are fun to sail in a pan or bathtub. They also add lots to a mobile or stabile.

Cork or potato animals and towers[2]   With various size corks and a batch of toothpicks, show your child how to put the toothpicks in a big cork, making legs. Put another in for the neck and add a smaller cork for the head. Then let your child take over and make any wild creature or creation he likes. If corks are hard to come by, use a raw potato, or several of them cut in various sizes.

Pine–cone birds[3]   Using a large cone for the body, help your child glue on a smaller one for the head. For the feathers, add wisps of bright paper or real feathers.

Coat hanger and thread—stabile and mobile[4]   Take

[1], [2] Unsafe for any child who still puts things into his mouth.
[3], [4] May be hard for three-year-olds.

a small empty carton. Turn it upside down and use it as a base for a stabile construction. Push the hook end of a coat hanger through the top of the box. From the inside, bend the hook back and tape it down to make the hanger fairly stable (or make a base for the hook with a large blob of play dough—(see p. 65). Let the children hang different lengths of thread from the hanger and fasten all sorts of things to the loose ends.

Try :

pine cones[1]
plastic spoons or forks
pieces of coloured paper
aluminium foil
biscuit cutters
shells[2]

MAKE BELIEVE

Children from three to six love to make-believe that they are almost anything from tigers to aeroplanes. But most especially, they like to pretend that they are grown-ups—lorry drivers, train conductors, firemen, office workers and Mummy and Daddy.

So when you're cleaning out drawers or cupboards, save some of your husband's old clothing as well as your own. Your small son will also enjoy pretending to shave with an old razor (with blade removed), shaving brush and soap. If his father carries a briefcase to work, he will have fun swaggering around the house with his own.

Boys like dressing up in parts of uniforms, too—police badges, armed services insignia, fireman's hats—as well as cowboy boots and hat. So do girls.

Boys as well as girls like to dress up in Mummy's skirts. This is perfectly natural at this age. If your son smears lipstick on his mouth, don't give it a second

[4], [5] Unsafe for any child who still puts things into his mouth

thought—except to save your favourite lipstick. This doesn't mean he's going to be a 'sissy',

Make-believe doesn't begin or end with dressing up. It is very strong in children of this age and shows itself in everything from daydreaming to playing with paints and clay. Puppets are another fine form of make-believe and 'acting things out'; so are storybooks. Trying to sort out the 'real' from the 'pretend' world is an important task of the three-, four-, and five-year-old. He's working at it all the time.

Kings, Queens and cowboys   For dress-up, here are some bits of old clothing both boys and girls will treasure :

WOMEN'S

dresses	coats	scarves
shoes	aprons	ruffled petticoats
skirts	artificial flowers	veils
any uniform	jewellery	ribbons
blouses	handbags	hats

MEN'S

shoes	jeans	badges
shirts	mufflers	caps
trousers	wallets	any uniform :
hats	armed services	police, doctor
work aprons	insignia	postman, military

Keep them all together in a big box for the moment someone asks, 'What do we do now, Mummy?'

OTHER GOOD 'DRESS-UP' MATERIALS

Aluminium foil   If the occasion is a very special one and you are willing to use this expensive stuff, you can make your child very happy. For a girl, crunch a circle of foil into a crown for a princess or a fairy. Cover a spoon or stick with it to make a wand or sceptre. For a boy, cover a hat with foil, then tear off two large sheets of foil, and put one against his chest and the other against his back, like a sandwich board. Crunch them together at the shoulders, tape them together securely, and he becomes a knight in shining armour! You can cover the top of a large soap box to make a shield.

Large paper bags   These make wonderful masks, with

holes cut out for the eyes. If he wants a fancy mask, a child can colour the outside, paste on wool for hair, paper for ears, etc. Be sure not to use polythene bags though for space helmets or for masks.

Castles, caves and aeroplanes   A chair may be just a chair to you, with or without smudge of chocolate on the cushion. But to a little child, chairs, tables, and beds can become boats or trains or a whole house. It doesn't take more than a small suggestion from you to jog their imaginations.

A bed can be a boat for a trip. If the children get off the bed, remind them that they are in the water and had better swim back to their boat.

A row of chairs can be a train or an aeroplane. Give the children some food (apples or buns) for the trip. A spare table near the chairs can be the restaurant car. Send them off with a few books for reading on the train or plane.

A card table or kitchen table with or without a bed-spread or blanket over it, can be a house or a cave.

A small dustbin of heavy-gauge metal makes a fine horse to sit astride.

Empty toilet-paper or paper-towel rolls make realistic horns, megaphones, and telescopes, especially if you wind coloured cellophane tape around them. Give your child one, with the suggestion that he play 'band man', 'sailor at sea', or a 'spaceman' looking at other planets.

Large cardboard cartons, three or four in a row, can be a train. The 'conductor' can use an egg carton to collect the 'fares' and give out 'tickets' made from torn-up pieces of paper. The 'vendor' can sell the passengers real magazines and peanut-butter sandwiches. Small bags of biscuits and raisins can be carried by the passengers for the 'trip'.

A paper plate can be a steering wheel. Then the row of cartons can become a car or boat. For variety : make a loop for a child's hand in a length of clothes-line and tie the other end to a carton. The children can then take turns pulling each other in the box, and get rid of excess energy while having fun.

Empty food tins and boxes make a fine play store. Save a big collection of old ones for a rainy day 'store'. Rinse them out but be sure to leave the labels on. Tear up bits of aluminium foil for money or cut green paper into 'notes' and use buttons for coins. An egg carton makes an excellent cashbox. The children will have a fine time pretending they're real shopkeepers. Some especially good tins and boxes to save in your cupboard or basement :

cake	biscuit	tea
salt	juice	coffee
fruits	soup	vegetables
baking powder	cocoa	soap powder

A sock can be pulled over the end of a broomstick for the head of a hobby horse. Stuff the sock with old pieces of materials and tie it tight at the 'neck' around the broomstick. If you like—and your child doesn't put things in his mouth—add buttons for eyes and a piece of red material for the tongue.

PUPPETS

Small paper bags can become hand puppets, if you help your child draw faces on them. A white bag can be a

ghost; a shiny bag could be a knight. If you make a little hole for the mouth, the child can poke a finger through it and make a 'tongue'. Two fingers may be ears.

Old socks and old mittens also make good hand puppets. A child can slip his hand into the toe of his sock and make the puppet 'talk' by moving his thumb up and down against his four other fingers. If you feel like it, sew two buttons on the toe section for eyes and another for the nose; a slip of coloured material may be sewn on for the mouth.

Potato and apple puppets With a corer or knife, make a hole in an apple or potato large enough for a child's finger. Stick on (with a small piece of toothpick) two slices of stuffed olive for eyes, or carve off pieces of the apple or potato skin for features, or use whole cloves. A handkerchief wrapped around the child's hand becomes the body, and he wiggles his finger to make the puppet move.

A hand can be a puppet With a felt pen, draw two eyes, a nose and mouth in the creases of your child's palm. By moving his fingers, a child can create all kinds of amusing expressions; if two children's hands are decorated, they then have four puppet characters to talk back and forth.

Doll's houses[1] Bought doll's houses seldom give a

[1] May be hard for three-year-olds.

small child enough room to play with her doll family. It's really easy to make a home-made doll's house, and it will be a lot better than one you buy. A doll's house can be open either at the top or on one side, in which case each room is like a little stage. You can make either kind from several sturdy corrugated cartons. (Wine merchants have the most durable kind, but the grocers cartons for heavy canned goods will do.)

With a small knife, cut out doors and windows on the sides. A one-storey roofless house makes it very easy to reach inside, but if your child wants a roof, make a removable one with a large, flat piece of heavy cardboard, or two or three of these cartons can be piled on top of each other to make a house of several storeys. This is best done with the open-side variety. If the box is wide enough and long enough, divide it with a cardboard partition, so that there are two rooms.

Your child can paint the interior walls of the house with bright poster paint, or paste on leftover wallpaper, or cloth. Small scraps of heavy material make good rugs.

Wooden cigar boxes, round cheese containers, and wooden matchboxes make sturdy tables and beds. Glue on match sticks for legs. Little cardboard gift boxes can also be transformed into bathtubs, beds, and tables. They don't have to look like the real thing. A piece of cloth will transform a box into a 'bed'; a bit of soap or sponge will make it a bath.

A doll family can be made from pipe cleaners and clay or from round-headed clothes-pegs (pp. 78, 98). However, the bought variety of tiny dolls of flexible rubber or jointed plastic are really more satisfactory because they can sit down. They are also easier to dress and undress.

Play Houses Huge corrugated shipping cartons for stoves, refrigerators and other large appliances usually make marvellous playhouses. Although you or your neighbours may not be about to buy a stove or refrigerator, you may still be able to get a carton from the appliance buyer at one of your local shops. Sometimes they are happy to give away the boxes of their floor models.

For a house, cut out a door and a window. Your child can paint it with poster paint and a big brush and then decorate and furnish it. Scraps of old cloth make good curtains. (Help him to stick them up with wide masking tape.) An old cushion or two will make a good chair or bed, and a few pots and pans give him a kitchen. If 'the house' is going to be used outdoors, it will last a little longer if you paint it and drag it under cover at night. The simplest way is to spray it with a spray-paint can. Do this when your child is asleep, because otherwise he'll want to help. Spray-paint and small children don't mix.

THE FALL GUY—A SPECIAL DOLL

At about the age of three, children enter a period of comparative quiet and not so many members of the family get punched, kicked, or scratched. But another idea—a very good idea—has dawned: hitting some*thing* is almost as good as hitting some*one*, and it doesn't get you into so much trouble. Punching or throwing a teddy bear seems safer than attacking a younger sister or a mother. Sometimes young children spontaneously pick on one of their own animals or dolls to use as the 'fall guy' for their rages and frustrations. They hit him, lecture him, and kick him around. Sometimes giving the child a special doll made for this purpose can be a great help to him.

Why are these rages necessary? Why can't children be taught not to get angry and not to hit anything? Learning new skills—how to throw a ball, how to use a spoon, how to sit at the table—is a difficult job and, often, frustrating. One of a child's main reasons for learning is that his parents want him to. He wants to please his parents, but it's a hard job. He has to learn to control his hand muscles, his foot muscles, his eyes, his ears, his bowels. Frustration and anger are inevitable if a child is developing. Unlike grown-ups, who can hit a tennis ball or go bowling or spill out their feelings to a sympathetic friend, a young child has very few outlets for his frustrations. But he can learn to take his anger out on things rather than people, and

that's a big step forward. Help him find ways to do this.

Many mothers and nursery school teachers have found 'fall guy' dolls work wonderfully well. Sometimes it's a good idea to make enough dolls to represent your whole family—mother, father, the baby (that's a particularly important one if there is a new baby), and the older sister or brother.

Here's an easy way to make a *fall guy*. From a piece of canvas, cut out a doll's head and sew it together after stuffing it with old nylons. Embroider features on the face with coloured thread. The hair can be wool sewn on to the canvas with a big needle. Be sure it is sewn securely so that it can be yanked a lot. These dolls don't need any bodies. Simply sew onto the canvas neck a woman's blouse, or man's shirt, or an old baby shirt. Choose the clothing that fits your family.

Against this 'fall guy', children can, without causing harm, get feelings out where they belong—in the open. Bottled-up feelings can cause trouble later. You'll be surprised at how well these dolls can work.

COOKING AND CLEANING THE HOUSE

They want to help Mummy Many jobs around the house are fun for children. They can be happy and busy while you work and they love to feel they are working by your side. A child of five wants very much to be useful and 'help Mummy'.

A three-year-old may not be much real help to you but he is often a very eager worker. Don't discourage him. Choose something simple that doesn't require precision or careful attention and something which you don't mind having done somewhat sloppily. He'll soon learn to master his trade.

Washing dishes is a real pleasure for most children, once in a while. Let the younger ones begin with unbreakable pots and pans, plastic dishes, or tableware. Five-year-olds can usually handle breakable things without damaging them.

Laying the table A child of three can learn to distinguish right from left by setting the table with place mats, napkins, and tableware. Older children can add the glassware.

Washing woodwork, refrigerator, stove, chairs, and counters is satisfying work. Give the child a bowl half-full of soapy water. Show him how to squeeze out the sponge, and then let him go to work. This will actually produce some good results, and many areas will be spick and span after his persistent rubbing.

Dusting and vacuuming are fun While you dust, let your child push the vacuum cleaner. When you need to use the vacuum, he can polish the furniture with the duster. Three-year-olds can begin to learn to take turns.

Sorting the silverware A child over four can straighten your tableware drawer, matching spoons, knives, and forks in small batches.

Washing vegetables Give your child the vegetable brush and let him scrub the potatoes or carrots.

Preparing vegetables All children like tearing up lettuce, shelling peas, breaking up beans. Give your child a blunt knife and let him chop up a potato. You can cook it or throw it away (it will please him more if you cook it).

COOKING WITHOUT HEAT[1]

Icing   If you're baking cup cakes, make a basic white icing:

¼ cup	butter
3 cups	icing sugar
3–4 tbs	milk
1 tsp	vanilla

Give each child a dab of icing in a paper cup and let him add his own colouring. He can then spread the coloured icing on a cup cake, decorating with sprinkles of chocolate or raisins, chopped nuts, or tiny bits of jam or jelly. (If you're baking a cake, the children can dribble leftover icing over plain biscuits and add the decoration.)

Instant pudding[2]   Children enjoy opening packages of jelly and instant pudding (no cooking required) and adding the cold milk or water you have measured for them. (You add the boiling water to the jelly.) To make the pouring and stirring easier for them, let them stand on chairs next to the kitchen table. Vanilla instant pudding becomes pink, green, yellow or blue with a few drops of colouring. Let each child colour his own pudding in a small paper cup and then decor-

[1, 2] May be hard for three-year-olds.

ate it with bits of marshmallow, Smarties, nuts, or raisins.

Lemon and Orangeade   You will find that children love to squeeze fresh oranges and lemons on the hand squeezer, and can add the sugar and water for a delicious cooling drink. With some help, they can fill an ice tray with real fruit juices and freeze them into cubes.

Salads   While you're getting dinner, the children can make fruit 'faces' on halves of pears or peaches. Let them decorate with cherries, raisins, slices of apple or carrot curls. Pear halves make fine bunnies if you show them how to stick in sliced almonds for ears and make cottontails of cottage cheese.

GAMES

Bowling alley[1]   Save ten large biscuit cartons. Take one regular-sized, unopened soup can, and you have a bowling alley. The children can roll the can on its side across the kitchen floor and knock over the carton tenpins. (Maybe you'd better put a pillow behind the cartons so the can doesn't crack the wall.)

Newspaper war   Let the children crumple newspaper into ammunition balls and arrange forts of cardboard boxes for a good battle. No one gets hurt and lots of 'fight' gets played out.

[1] May be hard for three-year-olds.

Broomstick and hat game   Tie a broomstick to the back of a chair, put an old hat on top and see if the children can knock it off with a dry sponge.

Circus toss   Cut a good-sized hole in an old sheet and drape it on a chair or table. Let the children try to throw a dry sponge through the hole. For a party, paint a big face on the sheet, using the hole for the mouth.

Toss game   Use big buttons or playing cards and an old hat (or shoe) box. Let your children see how many cards or buttons they can get into the hat.

Puzzles   You can keep one child or a group entertained for quite a while with magazine-picture puzzles. Choose one large coloured magazine illustration for each child and paste it on a piece of cardboard. Then cut it up into four or five pieces for the child to put together. When he can do it easily, exchange the puzzles. Finally, make the puzzles harder to assemble by cutting them up into very small pieces.

PLAYING WITH MUSIC

Singing and Dancing   A three-year-old can sing snatches of songs and will enjoy jumping around the room in time to music. By the time he is four, he usually recognises melodies and is able to sing whole songs. Because the four-year-old is so fascinated with make-

believe and is willing to take turns in group play, this
is the fine age to introduce him to those wonderful
old-time singing games such as 'Ring-a-ring-a-
Roses', 'Here We Go Looby Loo', 'Here We Go
Gathering Nuts in May', and 'Here We Go Round the
Mulberry Bush'. (Words and music can be found in
song-books listed on p. 170.)

If you can play the piano even a little, your child
from three to six will be an appreciative audience. At
five, many children can pick out simple tunes with one
finger—if you show them how. They can also begin to
produce crude rhythms in time to music.

Dancing becomes important to five-year-olds although they really are not ready yet for dancing classes
of any kind. With a little suggestion from you ('You're
an Indian', or 'You're a willow tree in the wind' or
'You're an elephant'), a five-year-old can crouch,
bend, weave, tiptoe and work out fairly elaborate
dances in time to music. Children like best to dance in
bare feet. A dance session in loose pyjamas and bare
feet just before bedtime is good fun and helps relax a
child for sleep.

Wearing a hat or holding something in his hand often
does away with self-consciousness and frees a child's
movements and imagination as he dances. Give him
some silk scarves, coloured tissue (or crâpe) paper, or
a large feather or leaf. Any hat will do (see goofy hats,
p. 121), or try a paper mask (see p. 103).

THE SOUND OF MUSIC

Almost all children from eight months to six years (and seven, eight, nine, or ten) have a marvellous time with these home-made musical instruments :

Pot lids   Two flat lids make a *cymbal.*

Flour sprinkler Put some dry macaroni in the sprinkler, tape the top on securely and you have a rattle.

Large empty tins   Easy to hold and bang. Be sure there are no rough edges. Leave the labels on or take them off. The effect is the same.

Wooden spoon   Fine for striking tins and lids.

Cardboard cylinders from paper-towel rolls   After

you've used up the paper, make the cylinders into fifes and bean rattles. For a fife, punch five small holes in a row down the top of the empty cylinder. Then cover one end with waxed paper and fasten it securely with sellotape. When your child hums a tune into the tube, the sound is amplified. By covering some of the holes on the top with his fingers, he can produce different notes.

Empty salt drums filled with a handful of rice or pebbles make good rattles or *maracas*. (Tape the opening in the lid securely so the rice or pebbles won't spill out.)

Empty circular cartons and boxes become drums and tambourines. Either tape the lid onto the carton with adhesive tape and let the child thump and shake the whole thing, or give him just the lid for a tambourine.

Empty paint tins with both ends removed make even better drums. Cut two circles, large enough to cover the ends of the can, from an old rubber inner-tube, and punch holes around the edges of the rubber circle and then lace them tightly to one another by drawing a string or shoelace through the holes and back and forth along the side of the tin. Plastic or leather shoelaces are best.

Hair combs covered with toilet tissue become harmonicas. They have a nice brassy sound. Show the child how to hold the tissue-covered comb against his mouth and sing or hum with his mouth slightly open. It tickles, too.

A shoe box with the cover removed and eight or ten rubber bands of different sizes stretched around it makes a *harp* or a *guitar* to be plucked.

Building blocks Tack or glue sandpaper to one side of two wooden blocks. When they are rubbed together in time to music, the sandpaper produces a shuffling dance-band beat.

Brown paper bags (or any other colour) make goofy hats for the band players. Roll back the edges into different shapes for the brims. You can lead the parade into the back yard to attract more recruits.

Records When choosing music records for the three- to six-year-old, don't overlook grown-up records, such as folksongs, classical music, jazz and rock 'n' roll (see record list pp. 171–181). A small child won't listen quietly to Mozart (unless he is a born musician) but it makes pleasant background music for finger-painting, and for helping a restless child fall asleep.

Whatever special kinds of music you like—jazz, African folksongs, opera, or the blues—will probably please your child, too. The important thing is sharing it.

The same is true of the 'activity' records. The first time he hears one, he'll love it if you go through the motion with him.

Story records are good for quiet times when you are busy and can't read to him. They are also helpful for children who are convalescing and must stay quiet. But the impersonality of a record can never replace the intimacy of your reading to him.

PLANTS AND ANIMALS

Even in a small city flat, a child under six can learn about nature. Scoop up a spider, some ants or worms in a glass jar. (If you're too squeamish, get somebody else to do it!) Punch a few holes in the lid to allow the creatures to breathe, and add a handful or two of earth, some grass or leaves. Let your child watch the ants and worms make tunnels and the spider spin a web. A magnifying glass makes the watching even more absorbing. After a few days, take the insects to a patch of grass and let them go.

PLANTS

How a plant drinks   Fill an old glass with water and some red food colouring. Then cut off the bottom of a stalk of celery or a carrot and let your child put it in the coloured water. In several hours, let him cut open the vegetable with a blunt knife. The celery will be peppermint-striped; the carrot inside will be bright red. This 'surprise' shows how a plant drinks water.

What else a plant needs   Let your child wet a bath sponge and sprinkle grass or bird seed over it. Put the seeded sponge on a plate and cover it with a clear dish. Leave it on a sunny window ledge and let him water it daily. When the blades of grass appear, remove the glass cover. After a while, put an opaque bowl over the grass. In a few days, see what happens. What does a plant need besides water?

Funny potato face   Scoop out some of the pulp from the top of a large potato and put some moist cotton wool into the little hollow you have made. Then slice off the bottom of the potato so that it will stand up, and put it in a small dish of water. Let your child sprinkle grass or bird seed over the moistened cotton wool. In a few days, if he waters it faithfully, the potato face will sprout a wonderful head of green hair. He can then make eyes, nose, and mouth with garlic cloves.

Roots are fun   Take a few dried peas or beans and

soak them overnight. Then show a child how to mois-
ten a piece of cotton wool and put it into the bottom
of a glass and add a few peas or beans. Soon he can see
the root tendrils spreading out through the glass, and
then the stems growing up through the cotton wool
towards the air and light. (Be sure he keeps the cotton
wool moist.)

Trees from seeds Grapefruit, orange, and lemon
seeds can be soaked overnight and planted in some
rich potting soil. If kept well-watered in a sunny spot,
they will eventually sprout dark glossy leaves and grow
into small trees. Or try acorns and horse chestnuts.

Onion flowers Put three toothpicks into a large onion
and then suspend it over a small glass of water so that
only the bottom of the onion is in the water. Put it
on a sunny window sill. It will send up graceful green
leaves and eventually produce a flower.

Eggshell gardens When you are cooking something
which requires lots of eggs, save the shells for a child's
garden. Let your child fill each half shell (nested in an
egg carton) with earth and plant a large seed such as a
zinnia or dwarf marigold, or a dried pea or bean (after
it has been soaked in water overnight). Keep the garden moist. Not all the seeds will sprout but at least
half of them should. When an inch and a half tall,
they can be transplanted to little pots and later planted
in the garden.

Pineapple Show your child how to slice off the top two inches of a fresh pineapple and let it dry on a saucer for ten days. Then you both can plant it in a small pot of damp sandy soil. Keep it moist and in a month, after it starts sprouting roots, transplant it to a large pot filled with sandy potting soil. This makes a dramatic and different-looking house plant, and who knows, it may even produce a pineapple.

Avocado stone This seed requires a long waiting period (often as long as six or seven weeks) but once it starts to grow, the changes happen quickly. Be sure you pick a ripe stone to start with.

First wash the avocado stone with warm water, then insert several toothpicks to suspend one third of it in a full glass of water. Put it in a warm place in dim light for four to seven weeks. Your child can add more water as needed. Tell him that the stone should split and start sending out a stem and roots. He'll be thrilled to tell you when this finally happens. Then you can move it to the light.

When the stem is about five inches high, you should plant the stone in earth in a big flower pot (at least nine inches in diameter). Keep it in a sunny spot and water it about twice a week. This experiment is best for older children. It's hard for younger ones to wait so long. Even older ones forget about watering in the long first sprouting period. It's more fun after it's sprouted.

ANIMALS

Most children even at a very early age like animals. But they can't be expected to take care of them until they are six or seven. Unless you have older children, the care and feeding of cats, goldfish, hamsters, whatever pet you get, will fall into your hands. Also, very young children have no concept of their own strength and the harm it can do. Many young children have inadvertently hurt or killed a baby kitten by squeezing it too hard. Until he is five or six, it is really too much to expect a child to gauge the difference between squeezing and holding very gently. So you will need to be with a child when he's playing with a baby pet and keep showing him how to hold it.

On the other hand, there is nothing like taking care of a living thing. Watching a kitten or gerbil or a goldfish play and grow is a wonderful experience in fun and learning. A five-year-old can begin to observe and question in a real way. What does a chipmunk eat? How does a gerbil make his house? Does the hamster like one part of the cage better than the other? Is a mouse shy? What do newborn kittens look like? For very young children, it's the watching—not the handling—that is the greatest part of the fun.

Home-made Bird Feeding Box If you live in the country or in the suburbs, your child will be able to watch many birds come and go. Even two-year-olds like to look out of the window and find a bird at the feeding box. Older children will notice the different sizes of the birds and will enjoy watching for the birds they see in bird books. But city children in large metropolitan areas have little chance of being visited by any birds other than pigeons, starlings and sparrows.

A four-year-old can make a bird feeding box. With blunt scissors, help him cut out two windows about an inch from the bottom of a small carton. Make the windows about two or three inches wide and about one inch high. (If they are higher, the seed will blow out onto the ground.)

Your child can cover it with heavy aluminium foil; paper, of course, will get soaked in the rain. Run a piece of string, cord, wire, or clothes-line through the top of the carton so that you can hang the new feeding box on a nearby branch. Put a handful of bird seed or a piece of suet in the bottom.

A few pets are both easy to look after and particularly suited to small children, but most mammals require special attention.

Cats are the traditional standby. They are fun to watch at play, especially when they are kittens, and they can be very affectionate—when they want to be, of course. Not requiring much exercise, they are easy to keep in flats. When you go away, you can often leave your cat with friends or neighbours without fear of complications. Most cats, like dogs, can take a lot from children, but there are some which, when pushed to the limit (pulled by the tail, for instance), will scratch. This attack can be frightening to a small child. (Be sure the child's tetanus innoculations are up-to-date.)

Dogs are a family affair—for Mother, Father and all the children. Everyone in the family should agree on the need to have one. Dogs need people for company and play—they respond to people more than most other pets do. It isn't long before a puppy is a member of the family, but he will need a lot of petting, patting *and* training. A family shouldn't take on a dog unless they can give time and attention to him.

Certain breeds are less highly-strung than others and can tolerate the teasing and playing of the very young. If you are considering getting a dog, ask a vet what kind he thinks is best for your children and your particular living arrangements. Some dogs get enough exercise on a leash in the city; others need to roam the wide-open spaces. Most dog breeders say that, if you are going to have a dog around small children, you should get the dog as a puppy. He should grow up with the children and be familiar with their play from the start.

Before buying other pets, get a book on the subject. Small mammals such as mice, gerbils and hamsters

are suitable for children but all need supervision and attention. It's no good keeping them if you are frightened of them yourself as the child won't get much fun either—and if you mind about the smell don't keep mice.

Mice cost 7½p or 12½p and should be of the domesti-
cated variety. They must be kept in an escape-proof
wooden or metal cage with plenty of ventilation and
light; the cage will need regular cleaning and the animal regular feeding with corn, seeds, hamster foods,
greenstuffs—and of course water. Your problem with
mice may be their rapid multiplication!

Gerbils are more expensive, and cost £1.25 or £1.50
each. They are slightly larger, more active and will
need a cage over 20 inches long. They are preferable to
mice, as they almost never bite or scratch hard unless
worried or excited. They are fun to watch and fine for
older children (five and six) to hold. They like to
crawl up arms and hide in pockets. You should be the
one to take them from their cage. Lift them out by the
base of the tail and drop them gently into your cupped
hand.

The wonderful thing about gerbils is their curiosity.
They are always bustling around their cage. Put a
topless glass jar inside the cage and watch them. Or
try an empty toilet-paper roll, some old socks, bells,
paper, blocks, a toy ladder—anything you or your child
think the gerbil would have fun with. Don't worry
about cleaning the gerbil's cage. Once every two or
three weeks is plenty. They make only a few droppings
of highly concentrated urine each day and eat their
own droppings. In fact, if the cage is cleaned too often,
it can lead to a vitamin deficiency.

Gerbils, like identical twins, look exactly alike. If

you have more than one, mark each one's forehead or ear with a dab from a felt-tipped pen so that the children can tell them apart. Older children can see how long it takes for a gerbil to change its coat.

If you have a male and a female gerbil, watch for a family. Babies are usually born in fours or fives, but sometimes a mother will give birth to as many as eight or nine. The babies are small, about the size of a paper clip. Adult gerbils seem to manage beautifully by themselves during the birth. The father gerbil stays in the cage during the birth and may wash the babies while the mother gerbil keeps them warm and feeds them. You might wonder if you should do something to help the mother and father gerbils. Actually they are best left to themselves during birth and for the next two or three days. You can help by seeing that the family is left alone, for at this time sharp noises distract them. Just make sure that there is plenty of paper or bits of rag in the cage so they can make a nest if they want to.

Baby gerbils are very delicate at birth and rarely does a whole litter survive. Explain this to your child as soon as you see the newborn litter (you may not know in advance that the mother is pregnant). Be sure to reassure him that this almost never happens to human babies. Your child may be very sad to find out that even if he is quiet, tiptoes near the gerbil cage and leaves the mother alone, still some or all of the babies may die. But the prospect of death is no reason not to get a male and a female gerbil, or any pet for that matter.

Hamsters cost around 37½p each and make good pets which you can let out of the cage indoors. Don't keep more than one in a cage as two or more are apt to fight. Like mice and gerbils hamsters like sand or sawdust on the floor of the cage and hay for their nests.

Reptiles, amphibians, fish and insects need less care than mammals. Goldfish make active pets but should not be kept in a bowl as this does not allow sufficient oxygen to diffuse into the water. You will need to get a rectangular tank and put an inch or two of clean gravel on the bottom with some water weed. Your problem here will be keeping the goldfish alive, but the commoner varieties are more likely to live longer than the fancy ones which are prone to disease. Be sure you oversee the feeding—many a goldfish has perished because of enthusiastic over-feeding. Children under six have little time sense and do not realise that the fish's last meal was just a few hours away. Goldfish eat fish food and small water insects such as daphnia. Keep the food on a shelf, bring it down once a day and show your child how to sprinkle it sparingly on the water surface.

Terrapins don't like too much handling, so they are best for watching, though their movements are rather slow for little children. Terrapins like to crawl up a smooth surface and rest on a rock out of the water, so put one on the floor of the tank. The little ones which cost a few shillings and are a little larger than a 10p piece are only a few weeks old when on sale in the pet shops and are apt to die in a few months, so it's better to get larger ones if you can. If kept at all they need warmth. The water should be around 70°F, as terrapins will hibernate and cease to be active in the cold. Feed your terrapin every two or three days on bits of raw meat, chicken and fish. They like all kinds of worms too and will nibble at fruit and greenstuff. Let them eat as much as they want.

Terrapin water sometimes carries bacteria which can cause an infection in children known as salmonella. After handling terrapins, children should wash their hands, and, of course, should not be allowed to drink terrapin water. Nor should any other pets.

If you keep a cat or dog watch him to see if he is jealous of your other pets. He might make off with a terrapin.

Newts make good pets and can be caught in ponds or brought in pet shops for a few shillings. You should keep them in an aquarium with four or five inches of water and put in a rock for them to climb on. They will eat small earth worms, daphnia and water insects. Do not keep fish and newts together as the fish may attack the newts if they are hungry. Your child can help you set up a pond-life aquarium for the newt's home with water insects such as water beetles, water snails and some water weeds. Newts can be handled, but if you get one out of the water for your child tell him to use a wet cloth or to wet his hands before holding the newts as dry hands can affect the skin.

Tadpoles can be interesting to watch in a bowl as they develop. Do not keep frogs in a cage as they do not settle down and can hurt themselves. They should be allowed, like toads, to live wild in the garden if this is big enough. A tortoise will live in the garden too, but moves so slowly that a small child may lose interest in it.

The death of a pet is sad but can be a valuable experience for a child, even a very young child of two or three. Because it may be a child's first experience with death, explain to him the real facts in simple terms and let him express his feelings openly and ask any questions—no matter how silly they may seem to you. The death of a baby gerbil or a goldfish may not be hard for you, but it may be quite an event in your child's life and one he needs help in understanding.

Be sure that you treat the death of a pet—any pet, a dog, a cat, goldfish, hamsters, baby gerbils—with the respect due to a living being. Don't flush the dead goldfish down the toilet or throw the terrapin out with the garbage. Children may worry that they, too, will be flushed away like the fishes or thrown in the garbage. Help your child to bury the dead pet (in a cardboard box) in the back garden or a nearby park. Even if your child is very young, bury the dead pet while he is there to watch you do it. This may seem like quite an undertaking on a busy day but it is particularly important for a child to make this connection with the realities of life and death.

WORKING WITH TOOLS

Around three or four, children yearn to make something real with the real tools that father uses—or with the real needles that mother uses. Both boys and girls usually love to work with wood because it produces something so substantial. How early they begin depends upon how much supervision is available. Many nursery schools let children start hammering and sawing at the age of three. But in a busy household, when you can't be close at hand every moment, it's better to wait until four or five. In any case, you or your husband will have to lend a lot of help at the beginning, and thereafter keep a watchful eye on their efforts.

For materials, you will need :

a small crosscut saw
small hammer
big-headed 2- 3- or 4-inch nails
sandpaper
paste
timber scraps, available free at your local timber
    yard (pick small pieces without jagged edges or
    knots, with the grain running *lengthwise,* as in
    wood flooring, to avoid the nail splitting the wood)
scraps of polystyrene

A good workbench   Nail two wooden planks (at least two inches thick) to a low table or two heavy wooden crates. This will be more satisfactory than a wobbly child's work-bench bought at a shop. A child learning to saw and hammer needs lots of elbow room and the table should be low enough for him to work comfortably (about two feet from the floor).

A good first construction is a polystyrene 'thing' with a bunch of timber scraps, glue, pieces of coloured wire, polystyrene, and other bits of beautiful junk. A child will enjoy making something of his own which stays together. Show him how to push large nails into the polystyrene with his hand, and attach pieces of wire, paperclips, etc, to the nailheads. When he's finished constructing, he may like to paint his creation with poster paints.

Hammering nails   If you're lucky enough to have a garden big enough to hold an old tree stump this is ideal for hammering practice. It helps his aim if the child holds the hammer by the middle of the handle. Show him how to hold the nail and ask him to keep his eye on it. He may hit his fingers a few times, but he's not strong enough to hurt himself. He'll soon get the hang of it and enjoy it immensely. (This is good activity for girls, too.) Inside, let him work on the floor with a long (to keep it stable) and thick (two or three inches) piece of soft pine.

Sawing   Soft pine is the easiest wood to saw, if it is

free of knots. You will probably have to make the first few strokes to get a child started. Then you had better stand by until he's finished to see that he doesn't hurt himself.

GIFTS YOUNG CHILDREN CAN MAKE

(If the sawing is too difficult, an adult can help.)

Blocks   Show him how to saw up different lengths of 2-by-4-inch timber. Then let him sandpaper, wax (paste, floor wax), or paint each block.

Plant or pot stands   Let him try cutting thin pieces of wood (such as plywood) into 6-inch squares. Draw the squares for him before he starts. When he's finished, he can sand and wax (paste, floor wax) them.

Bookends Let him nail together two pieces of wood (at least two inches thick, about six inches long, and four inches wide). This makes one bookend. For a second, make him repeat the process. Then he can paint them with poster paint.

REAL HARDWARE TO PLAY WITH

Magnet A child loves the magic of picking up pins, nails, or paper clips with a magnet.

Padlock and key[1] A big one is best. The key is easier to fit in the lock.

Magnifying glass to examine snowflakes, insects, flowers.

Discarded alarm clock is fascinating to take apart.

An old folding ruler to measure with. This makes a wonderful toy but a young child can break it fairly easily. Don't give him a good one you care about.

OUTDOORS

Your backyard may end up looking like a junkyard, but both boys and girls from three to six learn valuable skills, and have many good times with old inner tubes, rubber tyres (which make good swings but are also fun

[1] Watch out for the key if your child still puts things in his mouth.

to roll), empty metal paint tins, packing cases and barrels. Save old heavy plastic shower curtains and tablecloths for wigwams.

Constructions Four-year-olds enjoy constructing bridges and towers and then climbing to the 'very top'. For this they will need (in addition to the beautiful junk mentioned above) some long planks for ramps and some sturdy wooden boxes. After a boy has pulled himself up to the pinnacle of his structure, the ground may suddenly look pretty far away to him. If he calls for help, give him a hand but do it casually. Sometimes it's humiliating to a four-year-old to be rescued by his mother.

By the time your child is five, he will climb rope ladders, knotted ropes, and trees. You may shudder to watch him, but don't worry. He's surprisingly sure-footed. This age loves swings and stilts, too. Sandbox, mud, and water are still intriguing.

Painting[1] A hardware paintbrush and a can of water can turn your child into a painter. Let him brush with water the house, his tricycle, the fence, and even your car. It will seem effective to him because the object he paints will change colour when it's wet. A five-year-old may not be so satisfied with 'water' painting; he may want to do 'the real job—like Daddy'. If you have the time to supervise and an old shirt you don't mind

[1] Unsafe for a child who still puts things in his mouth or who may yield to temptation to taste the paint.

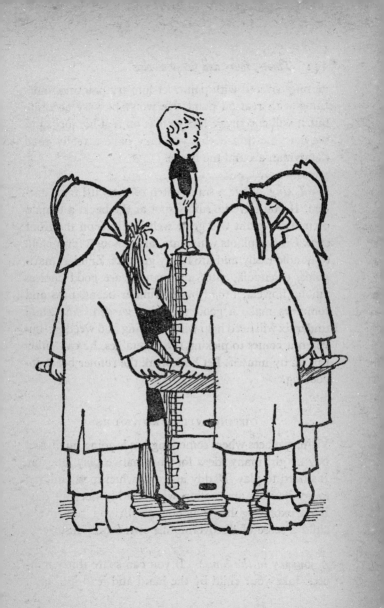

getting covered with paint, let him try painting something with real oil paint. He won't be very accurate but it will encourage him to take on real-life jobs, and by the time he's twelve you may have a really good handyman around the house.

Gardening Save a small patch of the yard for a garden. If you have no sunny spot at the back, a tomato or marrow plant will grow well in a tub on the front step. Choose plants which are large enough for a child to handle easily and are hardy growers. Zinnias, marigolds, calendula, aster and pansies are good choices among flowers; broad beans, runner beans, peas and tomatoes make a good vegetable garden. Any child under six will need help with watering and weeding, but when it comes to picking the vegetables, he can enjoy this all by himself. Let him break the runner beans for cooking.

OUTING WITH GROWN-UPS

Visiting places where something big is going on gives a boy or girl many ideas for imaginative play later on. It's hard to play 'Daddy at work' when most children today haven't any notion what Daddy does all day. Even exploring his own house with you can give a child a sense of discovering his own family history.

A journey in the house If you can spare thirty minutes, take your child by the hand and lead him on a tour of discovery. Talk about the pictures on the wall, a cherished vase, the begonia plant or Grandfather's chair. Explain what they mean to you and encourage him to ask questions. Poring over old family photographs or pulling everything out of an ancient trunk in the attic can be fascinating to a child. Sorting silverware together, taking special pains to compare the different patterns help him become more aware of beauty everywhere. A stroll through the back garden looking for birds' nests or worms, or looking carefully

at every tree and flower is fun if Mother is along, too. A child will appreciate half an hour of your complete attention and conversation far more than the most expensive toy or gadget you could buy for him. You are giving him something infinitely more precious to him—your own thoughts and feelings.

A trip to see Daddy at work This is an adventure which brings a young child closer to his father. Afterwards you can help make a 'Daddy work book' by tearing out magazine pictures and pasting them on pieces of cardboard. (Make these into a scrapbook by tying them together with shoelaces.)

Start the book with breakfast and follow Daddy through the day at the wheel of his lorry, or in the factory, classroom, or office, until he drives or takes the train home. On each page, write down his comments about each picture, based upon his own personal observations. In this way an important experience is translated into something a child can hold in his hands and relive.

Other ideas for outings are used successfully by many nursery school teachers every year. But they work even better with one child or smaller groups because they can be more spontaneous and can allow more time and space for wandering around.

A nature hike If you live in the country or can get there easily, try a trip just to notice the details of nature. Children often love looking at things closely and feeling new objects in detail. Don't undertake this trip if the idea doesn't give you any pleasure. You'll be impatient, and your child won't have much fun either. But, if you're the kind who likes to be out in the fields anyway, try looking at them from a child's point of view. He likes to see and feel the little parts of things, such as leaves and berries. And see how birds build their nests or cows chew the grass.

Unless you are an expert botanist and know exactly what is poisonous, don't let your child put any grasses or berries in his mouth. Teach him that it is important not to taste wild plants because he can never be

sure they aren't poisonous unless he grows up to be an expert.

You don't need to wait for sunshine. A gusty day with highflying clouds or a foggy, drippy day all have their special sights, and smells. Take along a big magnifying glass. Here are just a few of the *things that are fun to smell*.

honeysuckle	wild strawberries	clover
stink horn	dandelion leaves	wild blackberries
primroses	seaweed	cow parsley

What do they look like under the magnifying glass?

For touching and looking:

> different kinds of tree bark, from rough pine to
>   smooth
> beech leaves
> all kinds of grasses
> horse chestnut buds
> moss and mushrooms (no tasting)
> sea shells

What do they look like under the magnifying glass?

For watching and listening What are these animals
and insects saying to each other? How do they live?
Where are their houses? What do they eat?

birds	tadpoles and frogs in a pond
squirrels	dogs
cows	grasshoppers
horses	

Other places to visit The visits of three- and four-
year-olds are of the 'peep behind the counter' variety.
They like to visit small local shops. If you have a
friendly butcher or grocer, ask him if he'll let your
child go behind the counter and step inside the big
freezer to see the meat hanging. Construction sites
—big or small—are also an endless source of wonder.
Children love to watch the big cranes, the bulldozers,
the cement mixers, the wreckers, and the big trucks,
and to see the workers in their helmets. Other special
places are :

The post office   Early morning is the busiest and most interesting time to visit. Write a small note to your child and put it into an addressed envelope. Let him buy a stamp at the counter, put it on the letter and mail it in the proper slot. Then, if you can, go behind the front counter to see the workers sorting mail and cancelling stamps. Perhaps the postmen will show your child where they put the mail for your street. When the postman comes to your house the next day, your child will have his letter delivered to him. It's a kind of magic.

The fire station   Children will enjoy seeing the fire engines close to and finding out how the firemen do their job. Maybe the child will even be able to try on

a helmet. The time to visit the fire station is on their 'open day', usually in September, but watch your local paper for announcements.

The florist   On a cold winter's day when the earth is barren and grey, visiting a large greenhouse lifts everyone's spirits. A five-year-old with a passion for detail will like studying the flowers through a magnifying glass. A workroom where bouquets, baskets of flowers, and corsages are assembled makes good 'looking' and smelling, too. Why are the flowers growing inside the greenhouse and not outdoors?

The food factory   Any food factory is interesting whether it's ice cream, soup, or spaghetti popping out of pipes and vats. Canning and bottling factories are fun too. In large plants, there are often guided tours and samples to taste. Ring up first and ask about it.

The printing press or newspaper press   This usually requires telephoning ahead to discover when the presses are going to be busiest and if you may pay a visit. At big-city newspapers, a newsprint expert will usually be on hand to explain things. Children, especially, are fascinated by the trimming process. Be sure to bring home a supply of paper remnants for home art work. When the children are a little older, they may want to produce a newspaper of their own.

The police station   Not really recommended for very

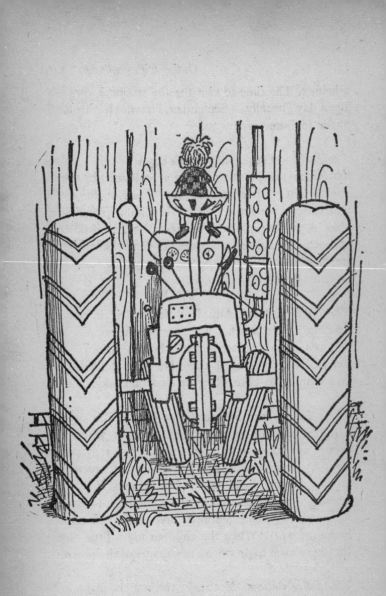

young children, especially in big cities where they are nearly always busy. However, many of them do hold 'open days' when all visitors are welcome. Find out from your local Constabulary when they are.

The Farm   A city child will especially enjoy visiting a large farm with a variety of animals, but he will want to explore everything thoroughly. This means watching the cows being milked and the pigs fed, climbing up the ladder to the hayloft, collecting eggs in the hen house. Boys will want to climb up on the tractors, too.

The pet shop   This is good for an hour's visit if there are birds, guinea pigs, rabbits, and tropical fish. Pet-shop owners are usually most hospitable to children if they don't bang on the fish tanks. Your problem will be getting out of the store without buying a parrot, monkey, or pet alligator.

The library   A children's story hour is a good way to introduce your child to a library. As soon as he shows any interst in books, see if your library has children's cards and let him choose his own reading matter (with some help from you). On a summer holiday, away from home, rainy days will be a lot more pleasant if you invest in a summer membership in the local library.

Other good places to visit:

   a tall tower with a view
   museums with special children's exhibits

airports
a busy harbour
a zoo
a railway station
journey on the underground (if this is a novelty for
    him)
ferry ride
buildings and roads under construction
cement being poured
road being tarred
big cranes in operation
power shovel
bricks being laid
telephone wires being repaired

READING ALOUD

A mother of nine once said that by the time her ninth child was born, she knew all the bedtime-story books backwards and forwards. You may, too. Even with one child.

At any time of day or night, reading is perhaps the best way to soothe a weary or frightened child. Or entertain a restless one. By holding him on your lap or sitting close beside him, a mother and child are brought close together by touch as well as talk, and, at the same time, the story provides entertainment for both. The bedtime story is the time-hallowed transition between the active day and sleep. Four- and five-year-olds are more prone to night fears than other ages and a reassuring book can make a great difference.

When you read to a child, encourage him to inter- tupt you and talk about whatever he likes. The stories and pictures may remind him of himself or his play- mates or the dog that scared him or something else that happened in his day. He may want to talk it over with you. Often a book will free a child to talk about some things that are bothering him that he doesn't quite dare to bring up directly. It's easier for him to say 'You see Curious George is scared' than it is for him to say 'I am scared'. This leaves you a good opening to say 'Are you scared? I get scared, too, some- times. What are you frightened about?' Many small worries and wild and woolly fantasies that upset small children are often laid to rest this way.

If you can, keep a child's books in his own room where he can browse through them when he feels like it. Even a two-year-old has feelings about the books he has. Library books borrowed over and over again can become as familiar as bought ones.

Three-year-olds often enjoy stories about animals. They don't have to be familiar ones—elephants and crocodiles hold as much interest for them as dogs or kittens. But the stories should still be kept rather short.

By the time he's four, a child is a much better list- ener. He likes funny exaggerations, but he is also a realist who is very much interested in the *how* and *why*. Pictures should still be clear and the text brief.

The five-year-old can follow action stories with good

plots. He also likes realism and fantasy (if not too frightening.) prose and poetry. He not only wants to be read to, but he wants to tell his own stories about something he has done or seen or may retell a story in his own way. If you have time, let him dictate a story, and write it down on large sheets of paper—a few words per sheet. Then suggest he makes his own pictures for it. He'll be proud of his 'very own book'.

There's a controversy over fairy tales. Many child-care experts feel that it's better to wait until a child is seven and is able to distinguish better between fantasy and the real world before reading most of them. *Hansel and Gretel, Little Red Riding Hood,* and even the *Three Little Pigs* can be scary with their cruel step-mothers and devouring wolves, and there are many other stories which are just as entertaining for children this age (see pages 157–170, for some suggestions).

BATH TIME

After an active day, there's nothing like a bath to soothe an excited child or comfort a tired one. Particularly in a household of many children, bath time can be a valuable period of quiet and private play. If your child enjoys the bath, try not to rush him through it, even though you may have other things to do. A child should not be left unwatched in the bathroom until he is at least six years old. Younger children can't be expected to be agile or alert enough to keep their heads above water if they slip and fall—or if they go to sleep while bathing. This means you'll have to be in the bathroom with him or in the next room where you can see or hear clearly that he is all right. Plan your day so that you can do something—tidy up, read or sew—*very near-by*.

In the bath, children really prefer to play by themselves. They like a private time to talk to themselves, sing, splash, soap themselves and day dream. The conversations you hear are a child's way of practising the complicated language he has heard all day; it's like the dialogue he may have with himself before he falls asleep at night.

Five-year-olds also like to experiment with water. In addition to regular bath toys, let your child try out a few household odds and ends so long as they are safe. This is a chance for him to begin to discover what water does to things and how things behave in water.

What happens to paper in the bath? To cellophane? To tinfoil?

What happens if you crunch up the tinfoil into a small ball? Will it float?

Why does the water go through the sieve?

Do soap bubbles last longer on cellophane or tinfoil?

Will plastic boats float upside down?

What happens to an ice cube in the bath? In a soap dish?

Does your hand look different at the bottom of the bath?

Children love to play with plastic containers that are shaped like animals. They will fill them and empty them, then fill them and empty them again. Which holds more water? Which lets the water out fastest? Which one can be filled fastest?

Sponges and sponge animals are fun in the bath, too. Is a wet sponge bigger than a dry one?

Put a few blocks into the bath. It won't hurt them. Do they all float? Even the big ones? What about plastic blocks? What things don't float?

A bubble bath makes the bath easier for you to clean and adds to a child's fun. He can blow the bubbles down to his toes and try to blow them into the air. How long do they last? Does a block float in bubbly water, too?

Appendix

CHILDREN'S BOOKS

SUGGESTED TITLES OF BOOKS FOR THE UNDER-FIVES

The following titles have been selected by the National Book League. Further advice about reading for this and other age levels is available to members of the League from the Education Department of the National Book League, 7 Albermarle Street, London, W.1.

ALBERTI, Trude, *The Animals Lullaby*. Bodley Head 1966, Illus. Chiyoko Nakatani.
A Japanese artist has painted peaceful, sleeping pictures to accompany Trude Alberti's simple, repetitive text about animals at rest. Difficult to imagine a better bedtime picture-book for the very young child.

AMBRUS, Victor G., *The Three Poor Tailors*, Oxford University Press, 1965.
An artist's version of a Hungarian folk-tale.

ANDREW, Prudence, *Mr. Morgan's Marrow*, Hamish Hamilton (Antelope Books) 1967, Illus. Margery Gill.

For children just beginning to read to themselves. The next stage is a Reindeer Book.

ARDIZONNE, Edward, *Little Tim and the Brave Sea Captain* (1936). 2nd edition. Oxford University Press 1955,
The first of seven books about Tim's adventures at sea describes how he stowed away on board a steamer, which ran into a tremendous storm.

AWDRY, The Rev. W., *Three Railway Engines*. New edition. Edmund Ward (Railway Series No. 1) 1949,
One of a very popular series. The youngest child will appreciate the pictures and the slightly older children will enjoy the stories which are particularly rewarding to read aloud.

BANNER, Angela, *Ant and Bee: an alphabetical story for tiny tots*. Edmund Ward (Ant and Bee Series) 1951.
An easy alphabet book popular with most young children. There are seven more titles in this series.

BANNERMANN, Helen, *The Story of Little Black Sambo* 1899. New edition. Chatto and Windus 1965.
The story of a little black boy, his new clothes and his adventurous walk through the jungle.

BARKER, Carol, *Rain and Shine: nursery rhymes for the four seasons*. Blackie 1966.
Nursery rhymes in verse, most attractively illustrated on every page.

BEALES, Joan, *Pip and The Six Cooks*. 2nd edition. Blackie 1966, Illus. author.
A very small first edition, published in 1964, went out of print immediately. Life below the stairs in a large

hotel is the background to this exciting picture-book. Pip, the kitchen boy, gives invaluable service to a visiting ambassador.

BIRO, Val, *Gumdrop and The Farmer's Friend*. Brockhampton Press 1967.
Gumdrop is a real car—vintage model: in this second story about him he meets a traction engine and only just avoids being parted from his owner for ever.

BISHOP, Claire Hutchet and WIESE, Kurt, *The Five
   Chinese Brothers*. Bodley Head 1961.
A somewhat unusual theme for small children as the five brothers face an executioner. But their magical properties enable them to escape an unjust fate.

BRIGGS, Raymond *comp.*, *The Mother Goose Treasury*.
   Hamish Hamilton 1966.
Hundreds of lively, humorous illustrations dance across the pages of this large book of nursery rhymes. Winner of the 1966 Kate Greenaway Medal.

BRISLEY, Joyce Lankester. *Milly-Molly-Mandy Stories*.
   New edition. Harrap 1960.
Simple stories about the day-to-day life of a small girl living in a village.

BROWNING, Robert. *The Pied Piper of Hamelin* (1845).
   Warne 1889, Illus. Kate Greenaway.
The legend of the Pied Piper who rid Hamelin of rats and, when refused his reward, led all the children of the town away into a mountain side.

BRUNA, Dick, *b is for bear*. Methuen 1966.
A simple, clear yet highly individual lower case a b c.

BURNINGHAM, John, *Harquin*. Cape 1966.
A story about a disobedient fox with a heart of gold.

To save his family he leads the hunt into the mire—
and the moral will stick as fast as the squire in the bog.
Sombre full-colour illustrations full of mood and
movement.

CASS, Joan, *The Canal Trip*. Abelard-Schuman 1966,
Illus. William Stobbs.
A picture-book for the very young involving five
tabbies who hide a persecuted Manx cat.

CLARK, Leonard, *Drums and Trumpets: poetry for the
youngest*. Bodley Head 1962, Illus. Heather
Copley.
An anthology of poems to be read aloud to children
with a second colour drawing on every page.

COLE, Michael and COLE, Joanna, *Bod and the Cherry-
Tree*. Methuen 1966.
A very simple story printed on small pages suitable for
small hands to hold.

COLWELL, Eileen *comp.*, *The Youngest Storybook*. Bodley
Head 1967, Illus. Margery Gill.
A renowned children's librarian and storyteller has
garnered a rich collection of stories and rhymes for the
youngest listeners—and early readers. A large type-
face and Margery Gill's honest line drawings give the
book a friendly, welcoming atmosphere.

Come Follow Me: poems for the very young. Evans (Zebra
Books) 1966.
A lively and interesting collection including nursery
rhymes in verse, lullabies, the seasons, fairyland,
Christmas and Easter poems.

CRESSWELL, Helen, *The Piemakers*. Faber 1967.
A humorous and beguiling tale based on the Denby
Dale Piemakers and the chronicle of their village.

DUVOISIN, Roger, *Petunia I Love You*. Bodley Head 1966.
Another adventure of that engaging goose, Petunia. What starts as a rather dubious friendship ends happily after all.

FLACK, Majorie and WIESE, Kurt. *The Story About Ping*. Bodley Head 1935, Illus. Kurt Wiese.
A simple story of a duckling and his relatives who live on the Yangtse River.

FOREMAN, Michael, *The Two Giants*. Brockhampton Press 1966.
A picture-book of distinction both in its exploration of feeling and in its graphic design. Two brown-paper giants have an absurd quarrel and until they learn to laugh together again the world they live in is cold and bleak.

FUNAI, Mamoru, *The Tiger, The Brahman and The Jackal*. Bodley Head 1966.
The Brahman finds himself in an unhappy position when he kindly releases the tiger from his cage, for that ungrateful animal has sworn to eat the poor man for his dinner. An ancient Indian legend, delightfully illustrated.

GALDONE, Paul, *Tom, Tom the Piper's Son*. Bodley Head 1965.
The version used in this book was published in London in 1850 and is from a treasury of pleasure books for young children.

GRAHAME, Kenneth, *The Wind in the Willows* (1908). New edition. Methuen 1959, Illus. E. H. Shepard.
The riverside world and friendships of Mole, Badger, Ratty and Toad of Toad Hall.

W.T.D.—F

GRAMATKY, Hardie, *Little Toot*. World's Work
    1958.
The adventures of a lovable and courageous little tug
working amongst New York's great liners.

GREENAWAY, Kate, *A Apple Pie*. Warne 1886.
Kate Greenaway's version of the alphabet rhyme which
is many centuries old.

HALE, Kathleen, *Orlando and The Three Graces*. John
    Murray 1965.
Orlando, the marmalade cat, is the hero of a whole
series of comic adventures.

HERMANN, Frank, *The Giant Alexander*. Methuen 1964,
    Illus. George Him.
Author and artist have imagined a good-natured giant
who uses his size to help his neighbours.

HOLLOWOOD, Jane, *Maggie and the Chickens*. Chatto
    and Windus 1967.
A pocketful of fun: this little book by a new author-
artist, tells how naughty Maggie, the gypsy girl, found
meat for the family's stew—and what happened to
Maggie when her father discovered she had been
stealing chickens.

HYMAN, Robin and HYMAN, Inge. *Barnabas Ball at the
    Circus*. Evans 1966. Illus. Yataka Sugita.
Glorious bright watercolour pictures show the adventure of a ball with all the circus animals. Short good
text.

IRESON, Barbara *ed., The Faber Book of Nursery Rhymes*.
    Faber 1966.
A new collection of stories for the very young.

JANNSON, Tove, *Finn Family Moomintroll*, trans. from
    the Swedish by Elizabeth Portch. Benn 1950.

Penguin (Puffin) 1961, paper. Illus. author.
A charming book full of fun and fantasy. Winner of
the Hans Anderson Award 1966.

KEEPING, Charles, *Black Dolly: the story of a junk cart
   pony*. Brockhampton Press 1967.
Glorious, fiery colours and realistic, almost three-
dimensional texture make this pony one the children
want to stroke.

KEEPING, Charles, *Charley, Charlotte and The Golden
   Canary*. Oxford University Press 1967.
A canary, bought by a lonely slum boy whose best
friend Charlotte has been rehoused in a skyscraper
block and no longer plays with him, is the link between
these two little Londoners. Georgeous full-coloured
pictures on every page. Winner of the Kate Greenaway
Medal for 1967.

KEEPING, Charles, *Shaun and the Cart-Horse*. Oxford
   University Press 1966.
A vividly illustrated picture-book about a small boy, a
carthorse and some stall-holders from the market.
Small children love the texture of these paintings.

LANG, Andrew, *Blue Fairy Book* (1889). New edition.
   Longmans 1949. Illus. Ben Kutcher.
Contains favourites from Grimm, Perrault, Daulnoy,
Asbjôrnsen as well as from English folk-lore. Other
titles in this 'colour' series.

LEAR, Edward, *The Jumblies and other nonsense verses*
   (1900). Warne 1954.
A selection of poems from Lear's compendium of
nonsense.

LEAR, Edward, *Lear Alphabet A.B.C.* Longmans Young
   and MacGraw Hill 1965.

LENSKI, Lois, *Davy's Day*. Oxford University Press
  1945.
Davy, being an American boy, has a slightly different
routine from an English child, but the situations are
familiar enough to appeal to all. First published U.S.A.

LINDGREN, Astrid. *Christmas at Bullerby*, trans. from
  the Swedish by Florence Lamborn. Methuen 1965.
  Illus. Ilon Wikland.
A delightful story about the lives of Swedish children
on a farm.

LINES, Kathleen *comp.*, *Lavender's Blue: a book of
  nursery rhymes*. Oxford University Press 1954.
  Illus. Harold Jones.
Coloured or black and white illustrations on every page.

LIONNI, Leo. *Swimmy*. Dobson 1966.
The tale of a curious little fish, whose brothers and
sisters have all been swallowed by a hungry tuna, and
his growing courage as he explores the unknown
depths of the ocean.

MAMLOK, Gwyneth, *Candy and the Rocking Horse*.
  Nelson 1965.
Bold colour and realistic illustrations in a remarkably
reasonably priced book.

MATTHIESON, Thomas, *First Things: a child's world of
  familiar objects*. Collins 1967.
Simple, colourful photographs of everyday objects
familiar to small children.

MAYNE, William, *The House on Fairmount*. Hamish
  Hamilton 1968. Illus. Fritz Wegner.
There should have been 2,000 houses in Fairmount
Avenue but the children could count only 1,999. An
enchanting story involving lots of children.

MAYNE, William, *The Last Bus*. Hamish Hamilton
(Antelope Books) 1962. Illus. Margery Gill.
Two boys who went to catch a wily kitten and their
dash across country for the last bus makes an exciting
story for children beginning to read for themselves.

MILNE, A. A., *The Pooh Story Book*. Methuen 1967.
Illus. E. H. Shephard.
Three of the best Pooh stories presented in large format with clear type and many new illustrations in line
and in colour.

MOLIN, Charles, *The Tea Party*. Hamish Hamilton
(Dormouse Tales) 1966.
Another little book, one of a series about the adventures
and mishaps of a bear, a tiger (with a zip in his back!),
an elephant and others written especially for bedtime
reading.

MONTGOMERIE, Norah *comp.*, *This Little Pig Went to
Market*. Bodley Head 1966. Illus. Margery Gill.
Rhymes, jingles and games for babies and very small
children, decorously produced.

MONTGOMERIE, Norah *ed.*, *To Read and to Tell: an
anthology of stories for children*. Bodley Head 1962.
Illus. Margery Gill.
A collection of a hundred stories to read and to tell to
small children.

MORGAN, Helen, *Mary Kate and the Jumble Bear and
other stories*. Faber 1966.
Quiet, short domestic stories permeated with love and
security; good prose ideal for bedtime reading.

Mother Goose and Nursery Rhymes. Hamish Hamilton
1964. Wood engravings by Philip Read.
A finely printed and designed book with unusual
coloured wood-engravings.

NESS, Evaline, *Sam Bangs and Moonshine*. Bodley Head
 1967. First published U.S.A.
Samantha (Sam for short) said her mother was a
mermaid but this was Moonshine talk. This book won
the Caldecott Medal in 1966 awarded by the American
Library Association for the most distinguished picture-
book and should make a point especially with children
who find it hard to tell the difference between Real
and Moonshine.

OPIE, Iona and OPIE, Peter, *The Puffin Book of Nursery
 Rhymes*. Penguin (Puffin) 1963, paper.
A collection which includes familiar jingles as well as
a number of traditional rhymes which have until now
been generally unknown.

OXENBURY, Helen, *Numbers of Things*. Heinemann
 1967. Illus. author.
A gay and exciting counting book which should keep
most under-sixes absorbed with its detailed and colourful pages.

PAPAS, *Freddy the Fell Engine*. Story by Peter Walsh.
 Oxford University Press 1966.
The beautifully illustrated story of a little red engine.
Other books by Papas include *Tasso* and *No Mules*.

PEARCE, Philippa, *Mrs. Cockle's Cat*. Longmans Young
 1961. Illus. Antony Maitland.
Awarded the Kate Greenaway Medal in 1961. Old
Mrs. Cockle, the balloon seller, grew so thin with
worry when Peter her cat disappeared that one gusty
day the wind blew her away with her balloons which
was how she and Peter were reunited.

PIATTI, Celestino, *The Happy Owls: a legend*. Benn
 1965. Illus. author.
A gentle story, beautifully illustrated. Try also Celestino

Piatti's *Animal A B C* which will be enjoyed by young animal lovers. First published Switzerland.

PILGRIM, Jane, *Saturday at Blackberry Farm*. Brockhampton Press (Blackberry Farm Books) 1966. limp

The latest in a favourite series of small books about the animals at Blackberry Farm.

POSTGATE, Oliver, *Ivor's Outing*. Abelard-Schuman 1967. Illus. Peter Firmin.

Ivor the Engine sings first bass for the Grambly and District Choral Society. Postgate and Firmin's humorous affection for old engines, Welshmen and music is catching.

POTTER, Beatrix, *The Tailor of Gloucester*. Warne 1903.

Difficult to choose which of Beatrix Potter's books to include in a list but there is no doubt that the tiny things in this one, like the mice under the cups on the dresser, appeal to small children.

POTTER, Beatrix, *The Tale of Peter Rabbit*. Warne, 1902.

One of the most famous children's books of all time.

RACKHAM, Arthur *comp.*, *The Arthur Rackham Fairy Book*. Harrap 1961.

Dick Whittington, Hop O' My Thumb, Ali Baba and twenty other stories.

ROSE, Elizabeth, *The Big River*. Faber 1962. Illus. Gerald Rose.

The chronicle, in words and in coloured pictures, of a river from its source to its sea-mouth. For the youngest. By the same author, *Old Winkle and the Seagulls* (1966) published by Faber in smaller format and paper covers, was a Greenaway prizewinner.

SEED, Jenny, *Tombi's Song*. Hamish Hamilton (Gazelle
   Books) 1966. Illus. Douglas MacDougall.
A little Zulu girl is entrusted for the first time with
money to buy sugar. The background is necessarily
slight in a book of this size, but it nevertheless brings
out the poverty of a society in which the loss of ten
cents' worth of sugar is a calamity. A series designed
for young readers leading on to Antelope and Reindeer
Books.

SENDAK, Maurice, *Where The Wild Things Are*. Bodley
   Head 1966. First published U.S.A.
A controversial and *avant-garde* picture-book in which
the emotions of a boy in a paddy are explored in terms
of a picture poem of great distinction.

SKIPPER, Mervyn, *The Fooling of King Alexander*.
   Hamish Hamilton 1967. Illus. Gaynor Chapman.
Bright, subtly-designed pictures and an economical
text together tell the enchanting story of how a wily
young Chinaman foils a wise old conqueror.

STEVENSON, Robert Louis, *A Child's Garden of Verses*.
   Oxford University Press 1966. Illus. Brian
   Wildsmith.
Stevenson's poems and Wildsmith's bold full-colour
illustrations recreate the child's microcosm vividly and
with precision.

STOBBS, William, *The Golden Goose*. Bodley Head 1966.
   Illus. author.
A beautiful bold and lively picture-book of the well
known fairy tale.

STUBBS, Joanna, *Shetland Peg*. Faber 1968.
A pony living on an island in the middle of the grey
sea has little hope of achieving longed-for adventure.
The delightful drawings show how her dreams come

true and make Peg a pony whom any child would
wish to own.

TOMLINSON, Jill, *Suli and the Kitchen Cats*. Faber 1967.
   Illus. Gillian Shanks.
A story likely to appeal to children and adult cat-
lovers alike, conveying something of the mystery of the
East as well as the amusing characteristics of the
kitchen cats and the splendid Suli.

UNGERER, Tomi, *Moon Man*. Whiting and Wheaton
   1966.
Large, intentionally un-beautiful picture-book about
the lonely man in the moon who comes down to
Earth for company but is glad to be catapulted back
into space.

UTTLEY, Alison, *The Mouse, the Rabbit and the Little
   White Hen*. Heinemann (Cowslip Books) 1966.
   Illus. Jennie Corbett.
Alison Uttley's books are well known by children and
their parents. This series is in a new, small format
which small children can easily hold by themselves.

WALKER, Barbara K., *Hilili and Dilili: a Turkish silly
   tale*. Bodley Head 1966. Illus. Bill Barss.
Adapted from a Turkish folk tale full of vitality and
wit with lively illustrations.

WELLS, H. G., *The Adventures of Tommy*. New edition.
   Longmans Young 1967.
A deliciously funny story, with the author's own
splendid colour cartoon illustrations, about a proud,
rich man who is saved from drowning by a small boy
and who sends the boy, as a reward, the largest, most
pretentious present he can buy—an elephant.

WILDSMITH, Brian, *A.B.C.* Oxford University Press
   1962.

Awarded the Kate Greenaway Medal in 1962. An alphabet book with coloured pages in splendid juxtaposition and excellent illustrations of cats, dogs, elephants, lions, peacocks, roosters, etc.

WILDSMITH, Brian, *Birds*. Oxford University Press 1967.
Rich paintings of groups of birds in which a feature of each bird's character clearly emerges. Pictures for the young child to absorb on his own. See also this illustrator's books on *Fishes* and *Wild Animals*.

WILSON, Barbara Ker, *A Story to Tell: thirty tales for little children*. Garnet Miller 1964. Illus. Sheila Sancha.
Short stories to read aloud to children from two to five years old.

ZION, Gene, *The Plant Sitter*. Bodley Head 1966.
Everyone has heard of a baby sitter—but what about a plant sitter? Tommy thinks up a new way of spending his holiday at home.

RECOMMENDED SONG BOOKS

The Puffin Song Book
    Compiled by Leslie Woodgate.   Puffin Book

The Oxford Nursery Song Book
    Collected and arranged by Percy Buck.   O.U.P.

The Faber Book of Nursery Songs
    Donald Mitchell and Cary Blyton.   Faber

CHILDREN'S RECORDS

Selected by Miss Margaret Davis, Education Officer
at E.M.I.

SPEECH

STORIES TO LISTEN TO

By Diana Ross

The Little Red Engine		
The Little Red Engine Gets		
a Name	HMV	7EG.8661

LITTLE BLACK SAMBO

From the story by Helen		
Bannerman and read by		
Ray Ellington	HMV	7EG.125

FURRY FRIENDS

Written by Alison Uttley and read by Majorie
Westbury and David Davis

Little Red Fox and the		
Wicked Uncle	Delyse	DEL.119

Little Red Fox and the Magic Moon	Delyse	DEL.120
The Squirrel, the Hare and the Little Grey Rabbit	Delyse	DEL.121
How Little Grey Rabbit Got Back Her Tail	Delyse	DEL.122
The Great Adventure of Hare	Delyse	DEL.123
The Story of Fuzzypeg the Hedgehog	Delyse	DEL.124
Snug and Serena Count Twelve	Delyse	DEL.125
Snug and Serena Go to Town	Delyse	DEL.126

PADDINGTON BEAR

Written by Michael Bond and read by David Davis

Please Look After This Bear	Delyse	DEL.171
A Bear In Hot Water	Delyse	DEL.172
A Shopping Expedition	Delyse	DEL.173
A Disappearing Trick	Delyse	DEL.174

BEATRIX POTTER STORIES

Dramatised with Music and narrated by Vivien Leigh

The Tale of Benjamin Bunny	HMV	7EG.101
The Tale of Peter Rabbit	HMV	7EG.102
The Tale of Mrs Tiggy-winkle	HMV	7EG.103
The Tale of Squirrel Nutkin	HMV	7EG.106
The Tale of Jemima Puddleduck	HMV	7EG.110
The Tale of the Flopsy Bunnies	HMV	7EG.114

The Tale of Johnny Town-mouse	HMV	7EG.115

STORIES WITH MUSIC

ONCE UPON A TIME ...

Fairy Tales by the Brothers Grimm and Hans Anderson told by Shirley Franklin and David Stevens. Incidental music composed and directed by Ken Rattenbury.

The Bremen Town Musicians; The Shepherdess and the Sweep; The Tinderbox; The Sweet Shop On Beat Street (Rattenbury)	HMV	XLP.50006

THE STORY OF SWAN LAKE

Told by Moira Shearer to music by Tchaikovsky	HMV	7EG.112

CAMBERWICK GREEN

From the BBC 'Watch With Mother' TV Series	Music for Pleasure	MFP.1109

CHILDREN'S FAVOURITES

Including *The Runaway Train; Doh, Re, Me; The Ugly Duckling; My Grandfather's Clock; In the Dark; Three Little Fishes; Teddy Bears' Picnic; Christopher Robin etc.*	Music for Pleasure	MFP.1175

NURSERY RHYMES AND ACTION SONGS

NURSERY RHYMES

Sung by Doris Gould with piano accompaniment.

Including *Sing A Song of Sixpence; Lavender's Blue; I Had A Little Nut Tree etc.*	HMV	7EG.8296

FIFTEEN FAVOURITE CHILDREN'S SONGS

Sung by the Michael Sammes Singers, with orchestra

Including *Boys and Girls; Baa, Baa, Black Sheep; Old MacDonald Had a Farm etc.*	HMV	7EG.109

MY OWN NURSERY RHYME RECORD

Forty-One Sing along favourites

Including *Oranges and Lemons; Ring A Ring O' Roses; See Saw Margery Daw etc.*	Music for Pleasure	MFP.1192

LET'S PRETEND—ACTION SONGS

Gladys Whitred and Richard Dawson with Orchestra	HMV	XLP.50005

SONGS FOR SINGING CHILDREN

John Langstaff and a Chorus of Children	HMV	XLP.50008

LET'S MAKE MUSIC

John Langstaff and a Chorus of Children

> Including *Frog Went a'-*
> *Courtin; The Swapping*
> *Song etc.*   HMV   CLP.3649

SINGING GAMES AND PARTY SONGS FOR
CHILDREN

Sung by John Langstaff
(with instructions on the
sleeve)   HMV   7EJ.266

SING A MERRY SONG

Sung by William Clauson

> *Sing a Merry Song; Spider*
> *and the Fly; Bamba; The*
> *Merry Old Sow; The*
> *Worm Song*   HMV   7EJ.259

LISTEN NOW

Sung by William Clauson

> *Listen now; Mr Cat; Peter*
> *and His Fiddle; The Town*
> *Musicians; The Woman*
> *Who Bought a Pig;*
> *Where Oh! Where*   HMV   7EJ.261

NONSENSE SONGS

By Edward Lear, sung by Elton Hayes with guitar

> Including *Owl and the*
> *Pussycat; Duck and the*

*Kangaroo; The Jumblies
etc.*   Parlophone   GEP.8551

PLAY SONGS

With Percussion. Arranged by Avril Dankworth

Including *Roller Skating;
the 5th November etc.*   Jupiter   JEP.OC40

**FIFTEEN SONGS FROM THE OXFORD NURSERY
SONG BOOK**

Arranged by Richard Rodney Bennett

Including *Little Boy Blue;
Jack and Jill; Little Bo
Peep etc.*   Jupiter   JEP.OC31

SONGS AND RHYMES FOR THE VERY YOUNG

Sung to Guitar and Piano

*The Postman; The
Dustman; The Milkman etc.* Jupiter   JEP.OC34

MUSIC FOR MOVEMENT AND MIME

LISTEN, MOVE AND DANCE

Record 1:
   Music for Quick and
   Light Movements
   Music for Quick and
   Strong Movements   HMV   7EG.8727

Record 2:
   Music for Slow and

Light Movements
Music for Slow and
Strong Movements   HMV   7EG.8728

Record 3:
Electronic Sound
Patterns   HMV   7EG.8762

Record 4:
Moving Percussion
composed by Vera
Gray. Electronic
Sound Pictures
composed and
created by Desmond
Briscoe in collabor-
ation with Vera Gray   HMV   CLP.3531

STORIES IN MOVEMENT

Music only, no speaking; story given on record cover
Devised by Rachel Percival

Record 1:
Persephone   HMV   7EG.8976
Record 2:
Beowulf   HMV   7EG.8977
Record 3:
Pantalone's Pantomime   HMV   7EG.8981

LA NURSERY (Inglebrecht)
    and
SIX SHORT PIECES FOR CHILDREN
(Arr. Gordon Jacob)

Played by the Jacques
Orchestra   HMV   7EG.8726

TUNES FOR CHILDREN

Record 1:
  Minuet from Fireworks
  Suite (Handel)
  St. Patrick's Day
  (Trad.)
  The Londonderry Air
  (Trad.) etc.   HMV   7EG.8575

Record 2:
  Trumpet Tune in D
  (Purcell)
  James O'Brien
  (Irish Trad.)
  Basque Dance etc.   HMV   7EG.8576

RHYME AND RHYTHM—NO.1: THE RED BOOK

An Anthology of poetry and music for 7–8 year olds

Recorded in association
with Macmillan & Co. Ltd.   Argo   ZRG.5414
                                      RG.414

PLAY TUNES FOR PERCUSSION INSTRUMENTS

Variations on Five Nursery Rhymes for Children's
Percussion Instruments by Avril Dankworth.

Including *What Are Little
Boys Made Of; Polly Put
the Kettle On etc.*   Jupiter   JEP.OC41

MUSIC FOR LISTENING

Peter and the Wolf (Prokofiev)
The Carnival of the Animals (Saint-Saëns)
La Boutique Fantasque (Rossini-Respighi)

The Wand of Youth Suites (Elgar)
The Dolly Suite (Fauré)
Hary Janos (Kodály)
The Nutcracker Suite (Tchaikovsky)
Swan Lake (Tchaikovsky)
The Planets (Holst)
The Toy Symphony (Haydn)
Simple Symphony (B. Britten)

GOOD IDEAS

Choose quiet activities for a sick or tired child; choose vigorous things for a child who needs to let off steam.

	Toddlers and crawlers	1-year-olds	2 and 3-year-olds	3, 4 and 5-year-olds
Alarm clock or radio	X			
A long journey through the house or yard			X	X
Bath time	X	X	X	X
Books			X	X
Building blocks				X
Colouring				X
Cutting magazines				X
Dancing			X	X
Fall-guy dolls			X	X
Feltboard			X	X
Finger paint				X
Furniture play pen		X	X	
Listening to music	X	X	X	X
Music		X	X	X
Nesting toys	X	X	X	
Newspaper fight			X	X
Oatmeal sandbox			X	
Pasting			X	X
Picture book without words			X	
Play dough or clay			X	X

	Toddlers and crawlers	1-year-olds	2 and 3-year-olds	3, 4 and 5-year-olds
Printing				X
Puppets				X
Puzzles			X	X
Reading aloud		X	X	X
Reserved kitchen drawer			X	X
Scribbling and painting		X	X	X
Sewing				X
Shakers made from salt containers			X	X
Shaving-cream painting			X	X
Shoe box and reels		X	X	
Singing				X
Soap bubbles			X	X
Sorting silverware, buttons, money and cards				X
Stringing buttons or macaroni				X
Tearing old sheets, paper			X	X
Washing vegetables				X
Washing woodwork				X
Water play			X	X

OUTDOORS

	Toddlers and crawlers	1-year-olds	2 and 3-year-olds	3, 4 and 5-year-olds
Digging		X	X	X
Mud pies		X	X	X
Outings		X	X	X
Paintbrush			X	X
Water		X	X	X

	Toddlers and crawlers	1-year-olds	2 and 3-year-olds	3, 4 and 5-year-olds
Alarm clock or radio	X			
Band or parade				X
Blanket		X	X	X
Bowling alley				X
Building			X	X
Chalk painting				X
Clothespegs (old-fashioned kind)	X	X	X	X
Colouring				X
Dolls house				X
Dress up				X
Empty shoe boxes		X	X	X
Empty spools (large)	X	X	X	X
Feltboard			X	X
Full tins and packets			X	X
Listening to records		X	X	X
Magazine paper chains				X
Magazine picture book		X	X	X
Magazine pictures			X	X
Magazine puzzle			X	X
Magic markers			X	X
Mobile	X			
Nesting toys	X	X	X	
Old sheet				X
Painting on newspaper				X
Paper-bag masks				X
Pasting-picture, collage with textured materials				X

	Toddlers and crawlers	1-year-olds	2 and 3-year-olds	3, 4 and 5-year-olds
Percolator, metal		X	X	X
Pie plates, aluminium or tinfoil		X	X	X
Play dough			X	X
Playing shops				X
Pots and lids		X	X	X
Puppets				X
Puzzles			X	X
Reserved kitchen drawer		X	X	X
Sandbox			X	X
Shaving-soap painting			X	X
Sorting silverware, cards				X
Special bag		X	X	X
Straws and pipe cleaners				X
Tearing sheets, newspaper				X
Threading reels, buttons				X
Train or plane trip				X
Wooden spoon	X	X	X	X

FOR A GROUP OF CHILDREN

	Toddlers and crawlers	1-year-olds	2 and 3-year-olds	3, 4 and 5-year-olds
Band or parade				X
Big carton house				X
Big carton tunnel		X	X	X
Blanket house		X	X	X
Boards and crates			X	X
Brush rollers				X
Building			X	X
Cake and pie pans		X	X	

	Toddlers and crawlers	1-year-olds	2 and 3-year-olds	3, 4 and 5-year-olds
Carton bowling alley				X
Colouring				X
Cooking				X
Dancing			X	X
Dress up				X
Dusting and vacuuming				X
Empty milk cartons			X	X
Full tins and packets			X	X
Furniture play area		X	X	
Kitchen help				X
Listening to records		X	X	X
Macaroni stringing				X
Magazine paper chains				X
Magazine pictures				X
Make-believe				X
Music	X	X	X	X
Musical games				X
Newspaper battle				X
Oatmeal sandbox			X	X
Painting			X	X
Paper-bag masks				X
Pasting			X	X
Play dough, or clay			X	X
Playing house				X
Playing shops				X
Playing trains, planes				X
Pots and lids		X	X	
Printing				X
Puppets				X

	Toddlers and crawlers	1-year-olds	2 and 3-year-olds	3, 4 and 5-year-olds
Puzzles			X	X
Reading aloud		X	X	X
Sewing				X
Singing				X
Soap bubbles			X	X
Sorting buttons, silverware, cards, etc.				X
Straws and pipe cleaners				X
Table leaf and cartons		X	X	X
Tearing paper, old sheets				X
Throwing games—ball, bean bag				X
Tin cans and old-fashioned clothespegs		X	X	
Washing woodwork				X
Water play			X	X

OUTDOORS

	Toddlers and crawlers	1-year-olds	2 and 3-year-olds	3, 4 and 5-year-olds
Blowing bubbles			X	X
Digging			X	X
Mud pies		X	X	X
Outing			X	X
Paintbrush			X	X

Index

*Below and on the following pages are details of
recent ARROW BOOKS that will be of interest:*

YOGA FOR WOMEN
by Nancy Phelan and Michael Volin

The link between physical and mental health is an
intimate one. The Yoga approach to beauty recognises
this. Designed specifically for women, this is a course of
instruction that deals with the problems of slimming and
improving the figure, increasing vitality and improving
the health.

Side by side with these physical gains will be the
development of a more positive interest in life and an
increased capacity to deal with its mental and physical
problems. The final result aimed at is a youthful, vital
look; tension and stiffness gone, replaced by suppleness,
a slim serenity and poise. Above all this is a practical
guide to a practical course of action, clearly written and
illustrated.

The Hebridean Trilogy

THE HILLS IS LONELY
THE SEA FOR BREAKFAST
THE LOUD HALO
by Lillian Beckwith

When Lillian Beckwith advertised for a quiet place in which to rest she received the following answer from the Hebrides:

Dear Madam,

Its just now I saw your advert when I got the book for the knitting pattern I wanted from my cousin Catriona. I am sorry I did not write sooner if you are fixed up if you are not in any way fixed up I have a good stone house and tiles and my brother Ruari who will wash down with lime twice every year. Ruari is married and lives close by. She is not damp. I live by myself and you could have the room that is not a kitchen and a bedroom reasonable. I was in the kitchen of the lairds house till lately when he was changed God rest his soul the poor old gentleman that he was. You would be very welcomed. I have a cow also for milk and eggs and the minister at the manse will be referee if you wish such.

Yours affectionately

MORAG McDUGAN

P.S. She is not thatched.

The Hills is Lonely, *The Sea for Breakfast* and *The Loud Halo* describe the unusual 'rest cure' which followed, and together give a complete, unsentimental, but often hilarious picture of life on a Hebridean island.

RING IN THE NEW
by Phyllis Bentley

The West Riding: setting for the earlier novels in the Oldroyd saga—the novels that were so successfully televised as the Inheritance trilogy.

Now the story is continued. The old closely-knit world of the textile families has changed. When old Henry Morcar dies suddenly, a new generation comes into its inheritance.

Syke Mill is threatened by a take-over bid. There is a protest march. Social conditions change but the picture of the West Riding and its people is as authentic as ever.

'A fine story magnificently told.'
Manchester Evening News.

'Deeply satisfying and richly enjoyable.'
Yorkshire Post.